Hans G. Schütze/David Istance
Editors

RECURRENT EDUCATION REVISITED

Modes of Participation and Financing

Report prepared for the Centre for Educational
Research and Innovation (CERI) of the Organisation for
Economic Co-Operation and Development (OECD)

Almqvist & Wiksell International, Stockholm

© 1987. Organisation for Economic
Co-Operation and Development, Paris

The Organisation for Economic Co-operation and Development (OECD) was set up under a Convention signed in Paris on 14 December 1960, which provides that the OECD shall promote policies designed:

– to achieve the highest sustainable economic growth and employment and a rising standard of living in Member Countries, while maintaining financial stability, and thus to contribute to the development of the world economy;

– to contribute to sound economic expansion in Member as well as non-member countries in the process of economic development;

– to contribute to the expansion of world trade on a multilateral, non-discriminatory basis in accordance with international obligations.

The Members of OECD are Australia, Austria, Belgium, Canada, Denmark, Finland, France, the Federal Republic of Germany, Greece, Iceland, Ireland, Italy, Japan, Luxembourg, the Netherlands, New Zealand, Norway, Portugal, Spain, Sweden, Switzerland, Turkey, the United Kingdom and the United States.

The Centre for Educational Research and Innovation was created in June 1968 by the Council of the Organisation for Economic Co-operation and Development for an initial period of three years, with the help of grants from the Ford Foundation and the Royal Dutch Shell Group of Companies. The mandate of the Centre was repeatedly extended by the Council. The present mandate is valid until the end of 1991.

The main objectives of the Centre are as follows:

– *to promote and support the development of research activities in education and undertake such research activities where apppropriate;*

– *to promote and support pilot experiments with a view to introducing and testing innovations in the educational system;*

– *to promote the development of co-operation between Member countries in the field of educational research and innovation.*

The Centre functions within the Organisation for Economic Co-operation and Development in accordance with the decisions of the Council of the Organisation, under the authority of the Secretary-General. It is supervised by a Governing Board composed of one national expert in its field of competence from each of the countries participating in its programme of work.

ISBN 91-22-00882-9
Almqvist & Wiksell International, Stockholm
Printed in Sweden by
gotab Stockholm 1987 85902

RECURRENT EDUCATION REVISITED

a 374
S 396

TABLE OF CONTENTS

Page

INTRODUCTION

PART ONE: PARTICIPATION IN RECURRENT EDUCATION AND WORK

I. THE CONCEPT, CHANGED CONDITIONS AND NEW CHALLENGES 13

1. The Concept 13
2. The First Fifteen Years 14
3. Recurrent Education and Recurrent Work: Obstacles to Alternation 18
4. Socio-Economic and Technological Change: The New Context 20

II. UNDERSTANDING THE PARTICIPATION OF ADULTS IN EDUCATION IN THE CONTEXT OF CHANGING WORKING AND LIVING PATTERNS 23

1. Recurrent Education: A Strategic or Descriptive Concept? .. 23
2. Two Approaches to the Assessment of Participation and Their Limitations 25
3. Changes in Working Time: Some Implications for Education .. 28
4. Other Changes in Work and Leisure 32
5. Some Conclusions 36

III. PARTICIPATION IN RECURRENT EDUCATION: A RESEARCH REVIEW 39

1. Starting Point and Purpose 39
2. Theories of Motivation 41
3. An Analysis of Valence and Expectancy in Terms of Adult Education 43
4. A Proposed Paradigm and Concluding Observations 53
5. Bibliography 60

Page

IV. RECURRENT EDUCATION AND INDUSTRIAL
DEMOCRACY 69

1. Background to an Analysis 69
2. The Educational Dimension 73
   a. Organisation and Control 74
   b. Process and Content 81
   c. Learning Resources 90
3. Issues for Further Consideration 94

PART TWO: THE ECONOMICS OF RECURRENT EDUCATION

Introduction: The Issues of Cost, Benefits, and Financing 101

V. THE PRESENT SYSTEM OF PROVISION AND FINANCING
OF POST-COMPULSORY EDUCATION 105

1. Scope of Survey 105
2. Provision, Cost and Financing of Post-Secondary Education 105
3. Paid Educational Leave 116

VI. THE COSTS AND BENEFITS OF RECURRENT EDU-
CATION 127

1. The Costs 127
2. The Benefits 130
3. The Economic Justification for Recurrent Education 133

VII. FINANCING RECURRENT EDUCATION: PRINCIPLES
AND MODELS 137

1. Alternative Financing Models for a Recurrent Education
   System 137
2. Criteria for Financing Systems Suited to Recurrent Education:
   A Critical Appraisal 145
3. Envoi 160

TABLES AND FIGURES

		Page
Table 1.	Trends in Average Annual Hours Worked Per Person in Employment	29
Table 2.	The Size and Composition of Part-Time Employment: 1973-1983	33
Table 3.	Adults' Motives for Participation in Education	44
Table 4.	Impediments to Recruitment	45
Table 5.	Results of Studies Comparing Participants and Non-Participants	47
Table 6.	Studies Supporting the Supposition that the Higher the Degree of Self-Respect, the Better the Performance in Achievement-Oriented Situations	49
Table 7.	Studies Showing a Connection between Childhood, School, and Work Environments and Self-Evaluation	50
Table 8.	United States: Participation in Post-Compulsory Education and Training Programmes by Source, 1980.	107
Table 9.	United States: Measures of Institutional Costs of Post-Compulsory Education and Training Programmes by Source, 1980.	108
Table 10a.	Percentage Distribution by Age of New Entrants in the Third-Level Education; University-Type Higher Education, 1981.	112
Table 10b.	Percentage Distribution by Age of New Entrants in Third-Level Education; Non-University Higher Education, 1981.	113
Table 11.	Germany: Public Expenditure for Schools, institutions of Higher Education, and for Continuing Education and Training: 1970-1985	114
Table 12.	Germany: Public and Private Expenditure for Initial and Continuing Education and Training, 1970-84	114
Figure 1.	The Expectancy-Valence Theory Applied to Recruitment in Adult Education	43
Figure 2.	Paradigm of Recruitment in Adult Education	54
Figure 3.	Design for Investigating the Expectancy Concept	59

INTRODUCTION

Towards the end of the 1960s, a number of new strategies and concepts emerged in national and international discussions of education, all developed around the central principle of lifelong learning. This represented a radical departure from the traditional assumption that active learning be concentrated in the years of childhood and adolescence; such a "front-loaded" organisation of education was seen to be obsolete in the modern world on grounds both of efficiency and equity. Following the lifelong principle, learning – especially organised education and training – should be available throughout each person's lifetime, implying the creation of new institutions and opportunities and the opening up of programmes hitherto reserved for a relatively small academic elite. The contribution of the Organisation of Economic Co-operation and Development (OECD) to this movement was the concept of "recurrent education" that was developed and elaborated in its Centre for Educational Research and Innovation (CERI). This placed particular emphasis on the need for organising education so that it can be experienced in alternation with work and other social activities on a lifetime basis (1). Recurrent education became a cornerstone of OECD's educational philosophy.

Despite the enthusiastic espousal in principle of these ideas and concepts by many of OECD's Member countries at this time, it soon became apparent that the barriers to the full-scale adoption of the lifelong learning idea were formidable. Established education institutions and systems were deeply entrenched and resistant to sweeping reform. The recurrent education concept implied too extensive changes in labour markets, enterprises, social insurance and income transfer policies – in short, the whole fabric of economic and social organisation. Moreover, the early 1970s witnessed the first faltering of the economic and employment growth that had been enjoyed in previous post-war years, and this quickened with successive oil shocks. The climate altered from one of expansion to that of caution.

In this context, considerably more than rhetoric and general concepts were required for the recurrent education strategy to remain convincing. Its further development needed detailed focus on the concrete shape of such a strategy, and the problems posed in its implementation.

Subsequent OECD work in this field undertook to fill out this detailed picture. This included a series of twelve national studies of actual developments and the implementation of recurrent education in OECD countries (2). Two volumes were published on the key policy of educational leave of absence (3). A series of reports on adult education in the latter half of the 1970s provided a comprehensive review of practices, policies, and problems (4). The response of the higher education sector to the adult student was the subject of more recent CERI analysis (5). And finally, three further areas became the focus of in-depth work by CERI, the results of which are contained in this volume, namely:

- Issues of participation – factors enhancing or impeding the participation of adults in education;
- Recurrent education and the world of work; in particular, the contribution of education to greater participation in the workplace;
- The financing of recurrent education.

By the beginning of the 1980s, radical changes were occurring yet again, with far-reaching implications for recurrent education. Structural economic change and particularly the development and widespread introduction of new technologies have re-emphasized the importance of human resources and the need for a broad, flexible base of knowledge and skills. For recurrent education, to the long-standing missions of emancipation and equality of opportunity have been added the crucial aim of developing human resources for economic recovery. We have attempted to reflect and discuss these new conditions in this volume.

Substantial inputs to this book were provided by Professor Kjell Rubenson, Department of Adult Education, University of British Columbia, Vancouver, and University of Linköping (Chapter III), by Tom Schuller, formerly of the CERI Secretariat and now Senior Lecturer, Department of Continuing Education, University of Warwick (Chapter IV), and Maureen Woodhall, Senior Researcher and Lecturer of the University of London, Institute of Education (Chapter VI and much assistance with Chapter V). Invaluable advice and editorial contributions were also given by Jarl Bengtsson, Viviane Consoli, and Ian Cox.

Hans G. Schütze
David Istance

OECD, Paris
January, 1987

REFERENCES

1. OECD/CERI (1973 and 1975), *Recurrent Education: A Strategy for Lifelong Learning* and *Recurrent Education: Trends and Issues,* Paris.
2. Published under the general title *Recurrent Education: Policy and Development in OECD Countries,* OECD/CERI, Paris.
3. OECD/CERI (1976 and 1978), *Developments of Educational Leave of Absence and Alternation Between Work and Education,* Paris.
4. OECD, Learning Opportunities for Adults:

   Vol. I – *General Report* (1977);
   Vol. II – *New Structures, Programmes, and Methods* (1979);
   Vol. III – *The Non-Participation Issue* (1979);
   Vol. IV – *Participation in Adult Education* (1977);
   Vol. V – *Widening Access for the Disadvantaged* (1981).

5. OECD/CERI (1987), *Adults in Higher Education* (forthcoming), Paris.

Part One
PARTICIPATION IN RECURRENT EDUCATION AND WORK

Chapter I
THE CONCEPT, CHANGED CONDITIONS, AND NEW CHALLENGES

1. *The Concept*

Recurrent education emerged towards the end of the 1960s as one of several concepts put forward as alternatives to the prevailing "front end" system that limits formal education to the early years of the individual's life. All these concepts took education as having a much broader scope than the provision made by the formal school and college system (important though this is) and posited that it should be available throughout a person's life – hence the terms "lifelong learning", "permanent education" and, of course, "recurrent education".

Though educational fashions and parlance change (and one may not hear any of these terms as frequently as was the case 10-15 years ago), it is relevant that, as recently as November 1984, the Ministers of Education of the OECD countries, at a meeting in Paris, reaffirmed their belief in this same principle of all citizens having periodic access to a diversity of learning opportunities throughout their lives.

Recurrent education is a strategy for lifelong learning that is distinguished from similar concepts by the emphasis put on the interaction between education and the principal activities and phases that make up each person's life – mainly, but not exclusively, work. It is relevant here to recall the definition set out in the first CERI recurrent education report in 1973:

> Recurrent education is a comprehensive education strategy for all post-compulsory or post-basic education, the essential characteristic of which is the distribution of education over the total lifespan of the individual in a recurring way, i.e. in alternation with other activities, principally with work, but also with leisure and retirement.

This definition of recurrent education contains two essential elements:

a) It offers an alternative educational strategy to the conventional one by which all formal and full-time education is concentrated in youth, i.e. between the ages of five, six or seven until entry into active life; and it proposes to spread post-compulsory education over the full lifespan of the individual. Thus it accepts the principle of lifelong learning.

b) It proposes a frame within which lifelong learning will be organised, this being the alternation and effective interaction between education, as a structured learning situation, and other social activities during which learning occurs (1).

After the fifteen years or so during which the OECD has been fostering this strategy, the time has undoubtedly come to assess progress towards its realisation (2). This will be an artificial exercise, however, unless proper account is taken of the nature and scale of social and economic change over this period. The climate of reform that coloured the 1960s has been succeeded by one of greater caution and retrenchment – more realistic, perhaps, but less conducive to radical reforms. Seemingly limitless economic growth and relatively full employment have given way to prolonged labour market difficulties, consequent upon structural economic change. The 1980s are typified by financial constraints and, in many OECD countries, education now suffers a declining share of the public purse.

These changes have clearly been crucial to the progress of recurrent education and, as will be argued presently, they have introduced formidable obstacles to "alternation" – the conceptual linchpin of the original 1973 CERI formulation. More recent experience has thus necessitated rethinking of certain features and emphases of the recurrent education concept. It is stressed, however, that the rapidity and nature of these social and economic changes have strengthened, not weakened, the arguments in support of this strategy, even if it has become more difficult to implement it.

2. *The First Fifteen Years*

No one pattern of educational development is typical of all OECD countries but whatever the structure and content of the existing system, progress towards recurrent education over the last fifteen years has undoubtedly been chequered.

In certain fundamental respects, the "front-end" model of formal education has been strengthened as young people, faced by a drastic decline in job opportunities and aware of the necessity to acquire diplomas in the sharp competition for scarce jobs, stay longer at school. Some countries have extended compulsory education (full-time or part-time) to the age of 18 (Germany, Belgium); in other countries, some nine out of ten 17-year-olds stay in school and college education (Japan, Norway, Sweden, United States). The concept of a "youth guarantee", ensuring for young people at the "transition stage" a real opportunity of either work experience, more education, or vocational training, has been put into practice in several cases, notably in the Nordic countries (3). Particularly in the face of high levels of unemployment, extensive efforts have been made by both education and labour market authorities to give youngsters, especially the 16 to 19-year-olds, greater access to education and training. Many of these initiatives display some features of recurrence but, by and large, they can also be seen as strengthening the "front-end" organisation of educational systems.

This trend is similarly reflected in public spending on education. Although most of the children born in the "baby boom" of the 1950s and 1960s have entered adult life, and there has been a sharp drop in the numbers attending school in many countries, cuts in public spending have been most sharply felt in higher and adult education. The share of resources going to schools has remained fairly constant, and the proportion of funds allocated to pre-primary and vocational education has increased. Widespread current interest in the quality of school education (4) underlines further that parents continue to want their children to be given the soundest possible start in life – a constant of education that has been little affected by the theoretical arguments for its reorganisation along recurrent lines.

The picture, however, is not necessarily a gloomy one for the future of recurrent education. The sharp contrast between the "front-end" and "lifelong" principles of education, while a useful heuristic device, has probably been exaggerated, particularly by the early advocates of recurrent education. It was never very likely, and the prospect looks still more remote with the passage of time that schooling and education for the young would recede in importance as developments to allow adults periodic access to organised learning have gathered pace. Nor is there any logical contradiction between the existence of a strong school sector and widespread opportunities for recurrent education. Indeed, each person should achieve the soundest possible start in life. It is almost a truism in this field that adults with the most extensive initial education are much more likely to avail themselves of learning opportunities throughout their lives than those who had a shorter and less successful school career.

Distrust of a strong school system by those advocating recurrent education has nevertheless derived from two main (and justifiable) fears: first, that schools function as very powerful vehicles of educational and social selection; second, that, because schools are exclusively learning institutions, they tend to relegate innovative, non-formal developments to secondary status. These fears, though justified, have begun to be overtaken by recent developments as a variety of extra-school provisions, many of them outside formal education, have grown in importance.

In fact, educational developments give grounds for optimism that progress towards recurrent education is occurring. There has been a considerable increase in individual demand for education later on in life, while different kinds of post-secondary and adult education institutions have responded in innovative ways through short courses and modular systems as well as by changing rigid admission requirements – including, in some cases, the recognition of work experience as a qualification in its own right. (These developments have not always been caused by a spontaneous concern for the non-traditional student, of course. With financial constraints and demographic shifts, the very survival of some programmes and institutions depends upon their ability to attract new types of student, notably adults).

The physical availability of educational facilities has increased with the establishment of new institutions and in the development of non-traditional kinds of education, so that geographical and temporal constraints have become less severe. The growth of distance learning through the mass media and other technical developments, and pressure on community educators to allow round-the-clock use of facilities, have also contributed to the expansion of learning opportunities.

The growth of part-time studies by adults is an important development. In the United States, some 60 per cent of students aged 25 and over are enrolled in degree programmes part-time, and in Australia and Canada this proportion is even greater (71 and 76 per cent respectively). Even in Europe, where full-time study is traditionally the dominant mode, part-time studies have gained in importance so that 45 per cent of mature students in the United Kingdom are now following courses part-time (5).

Paid educational leave was identified in the 1973 CERI report as one of the main instruments for the implementation of recurrent education by enabling working adults to enrol in education and training courses away from employers' premises, in subjects of their own choosing. It has been established in a number of OECD countries, but generally it has not come up to its full potential nor to the original expectations. This is due to a variety of factors, some of which are discussed in Chapter VI. Nevertheless, it remains one of the principal mechanisms to realise genuine alternation between work and education.

What happens at the lower secondary and, particularly, upper levels of secondary education is critical for the recurrent strategy. How many students lose forever any desire for further learning at this stage? With the diplomas of upper secondary education crucial stepping stones to the job market, what opportunities exist for those who have left the system to return and acquire them? Particularly with present high levels of unemployment, these questions have become increasing preoccupations of policy makers (6). One result has been the markedly greater emphasis upon vocational education and training – these branches have grown, absolutely and relatively, in almost all OECD countries (Germany, with its apprenticeship sector already so strongly developed, is an exception and here general branches have expanded). Many such changes are of considerable interest for recurrent education since they contain elements of "de-schooling" upper-secondary schools (at least to some degree) and a blurring of the boundaries between education and its external environment, especially the workplace.

Innovative approaches at the upper secondary level include: the upgrading or development of certain vocational branches with a stronger academic basis; the more flexible combinations of work and study; the introduction of compulsory work experience into academic lines; the development of non-academic, general courses that are more strongly geared to preparation for working life; the move away from "schools for children" for the 16-19 year-old group towards more adult institutions that may also cater for older students in post-secondary education. Another avenue being explored involves the establishment of more direct links with the community, e.g. youth service, community colleges, and co-operative programmes of various types.

Though each of these may seek to blur certain rigid boundaries – between education and work, between schooling and training, and between education and the community – differentiation in status and perceived value between programmes persists, and may even have increased. This raises the serious problems of selection and inequality of opportunity. The upper secondary stage of education and training is being assigned greater responsibility for the orientation, allocation, and selection of students, increasingly postponed from the latter years of the compulsory stage. And, as more of the 16-19 age group continue in post-compulsory education, those who drop out beforehand or who do not complete their course to acquire a qualification suffer still higher risk of stigma and disadvantage.

These particular developments illustrate just how difficult it is to achieve an equitable system of education reorganised along recurrent lines – a consideration that applies no less to higher education. We have already referred to positive changes towards recurrence taking place there, but provisions (and entry qualifications) are often uneven and frequently separate from programmes for the traditional student. External and extramural courses have thus suffered from the reputation of lower quality and value, though there have been considerable improvements lately.

The emergence of these diverse forms of differentiation may well be the inevitable consequence of inequalities of talents and opportunities as well as of scarce resources, but by no means should it be seen as a necessary obstacle to the furtherance of the "recurrent mode". Rather it should argue for the establishment of more extensive "second-chance" opportunities so that doors do not remain forever closed after the choice to leave education is made at the age of 16, 17, 18 or 19.

There are some grounds for caution, therefore, but they should not obscure the importance of the advances that have been made. In a time span that is brief by any normal standards of educational change, there has been a significant loosening of the dominant assumption that education must be provided in formal schools and colleges under the responsibility of the public education authorities. Other public authorities, such as those responsible for employment and the labour market, are now prominently involved in the provision of learning, and it is more widely recognised that there are many appropriate educational settings beyond the ordinary school or college, including the home and the workplace. Moreover, new initiatives and arrangements, especially at the post-compulsory level, have demonstrated the potential for flexible *combinations* of work and education, of community and school initiatives, of formal and non-formal arrangements, and of education and labour market authority programmes. Even if these innovative programmes sometimes appear to be peripheral, their influence upon prevailing attitudes and assumptions about education may well prove to be far-reaching.

This brief account of past experience reveals that the strategy of recurrent education should now be envisaged in rather different terms from those employed in the early 1970s. Then, there was an underlying assumption that involvement in all education should be like going to school. Recurrent education was envisaged as a *system* typified by full-time education in alternation with full-time work, and by implication under the co-ordinated direction of a public, decision-making authority [though other arrangements were not explicitly ruled out at the time, as Kallen has explained more recently (7)].

This is no longer a plausible guide to the reorganisation of education. "Front-end schooling" and recurrent education exist side by side. Recurrent developments take place in a bewildering variety of settings, under quite different authorities. Modes of learning – including part-time and distance learning – depart significantly from the full-time attendance typical of the school pupil. This is not to say that current developments are unproblematic: overall planning is increasingly difficult and there are often unfilled gaps of provision. But this does not alter the reality that the types of provision that come within the recurrent education strategy are highly diverse, come under different decision-making authorities, and embrace many types of student and modes of learning.

3. *Recurrent Education and Recurrent Work: Obstacles to Alternation*

Certain obstacles to recurrent education lie in education systems – notably, restricted access to higher education, or the absence of part-time provision, of evening courses, of credit transfer systems, and of distance education opportunities, or the habitual restriction of student aid schemes to full-time, academic courses. Students who make traditional choices are often regarded in the recurrent education literature as irrational, choosing early and unwisely rather than later with the wisdom of experience. To be sure, educational institutions are often slow in moving towards lifelong learning. But should the blame all be laid at education's door? Are traditional choices really irrational, given the world that the young person is about to enter? The answer to both questions at present must, all too often, be no. Recurrent education implies recurrent work. And this is still not the pattern chosen by, and available for, most people.

For recurrent education and training to be widely perceived as relevant by young people would depend on at least three basic conditions being met. First, there would have to be employment opportunities readily available for those who complete compulsory school and who do not wish immediately to pursue further education and training. Second, career ladders and training opportunities would have to be provided in conjunction with such jobs. Third, participation in, and completion of, education or training programmes at a later point would have to provide occupational advancement and income commensurate with degrees or professional qualifications acquired in the traditional fashion, i.e. prior to entry into the labour force (8).

These conditions are still far from met. Jobs are scarce for school-leavers and unemployment is particularly high among those who have nothing more than a secondary school-leaving certificate. This is a powerful disincentive for those who would like to postpone formal higher education or training. Entry-level jobs of the kind normally available to school-leavers are usually "dead-end" positions that demand few skills and consequently offer little opportunity to learn; on the contrary, firms tend to offer training to those who already possess professional or academic qualifications, and this is a further incentive to complete education before starting work. No assessment of "recurrent work", as distinct from recurrent education, can ignore the severe deterioration of labour market conditions and job opportunities since the latter concept was first mooted. Not only are there now over 30 million unemployed in OECD countries but increasingly adults are found in secondary labour market jobs with work schedules where training and educational leave of absence are not readily available nor easily implemented.

This again shows that the relatively straightforward "alternation" concept of the early 1970s has limitations. It cannot easily accommodate the many who are either without work, or who work intermittently, part-time, during unsocial hours or who enjoy little of the protection or benefits of labour market legislation. To be sure, there are many high-skill demanding jobs, but there remain large numbers that are low-skilled. Labour markets have seen an influx of young people and migrants, for example, many of whom have had to accept unstable and poorly-paid, often marginal, work. And part-time employment dominated by female workers has grown – typically poorly paid, without fringe benefits, and, in some countries, not covered by employment protection legislation (see Chapter II). Yet it can hardly be concluded that education is less relevant for these groups; the opposite is true. Indeed, as "untypical" working patterns become increasingly typical, the arguments for innovative combinations of education with other activities – recurrent education – become more compelling, for both social and economic reasons.

The challenge is, therefore, how education can be made available to the many for whom it is, at present, unattractive or unavailable, when it will neither result necessarily in increased profits to an enterprise nor necessarily be part of an established career path with training as an integral component. The challenge becomes all the more urgent as signs gather of the growing social duality of modern economies, with the glaring inequity and divisiveness that this entails.

4. Socio-Economic and Technological Change: The New Context

Discussion of the implications for recurrent education of economic and social change becomes more matter of fact when we bring in one of the major factors behind it – technology and technological change. New technical systems, in particular those based on the microprocessor and on telecommunication technology, are penetrating virtually all sectors of the economy in the OECD countries, and at a speed that makes any precise analysis of their future effects on, for example, employment or productivity impossible at present. Some maintain that technological innovation will enhance economic growth and overall development so that present job losses in some sectors will be more than offset by job creation in others. Others emphasize the labour-saving effects of the new technologies and point out that there is ample evidence that the extensive use to which microprocessors are put is primarily to rationalise, i.e. to reduce the workforce and thus wage costs. The rise of the "dual" economy lends some credibility to the latter view.

Increased non-work time, as one result of technological change in the workplace, provides an important opportunity for the participation of adults in education and training activities outside working hours, and this is discussed in more detail in Chapter II. Equally important is the influence that new technologies are likely to have on the skills and knowledge that are required from employees at the workplace. Issues of workplace reorganisation and democracy are wide-ranging, as Chapter IV shows. The concern of workers for more human working conditions and their quest for shared responsibility, on the one hand, and the interest of management to mobilise fully the productivity potential of modern technology, on the other, have already led to important changes in factory organisation, industrial relations and human resource management. New principles have emerged regarding the apportionment of tasks within and between work units in production, management, and engineering, leading to improved co-operation within enterprises. The establishment of new channels of communication, such as shop councils, quality circles, expression groups, is also intended to ease co-operation on the shop floor and, at the same time, to encourage innovative ideas for the improvement of work processes and the quality of products. These have extensive implications for learning.

A survey of industry commissioned by the European Community lists a number of general qualities likely to be required of workers on computer-based systems or equipment. These include: the ability for analytic thinking applied to different processes of work; a quantitative appreciation of different processes; the ability to conduct dialogue with equipment; a sense of responsibility and a capacity for autonomous work; the ability to link technical, economic, and social considerations in the appreciation of equipment and working methods; a planned and methodical approach to work (9).

Knowledge of the computer as a tool for managing and providing access to large quantities of information is increasingly important. Some even argue that "technological literacy" should describe a level of understanding of different aspects of technology that goes well beyond a simple familiarity with computers. A recent major study in the United States suggests that technological literacy will soon be required of all members of the workforce as more extensive applications of information technology are made in offices and plants (10). According to this view, basic electronics and informatics expertise will be crucial for the majority of jobs, together with general capabilities, broad basic knowledge and skills, the ability to learn, flexibility, and ability to think in terms of abstract, complex systems.

While opinions may converge on the skills required of those with a substantial degree of discretion over the use of technical processes in their work, a much less optimistic picture emerges, however, for the majority of workers. Computer-based processes might not only take over many intellectual elements of work (such as co-ordination, monitoring, and product control) but they might also lead to further parcellisation of work. Through automation, some assert, many of the skilled jobs currently requiring long experience and training will be reduced to easily learned, machine-tending tasks. Some even predict a "polarisation" where a minority of the workforce is confronted with increasingly complex tasks, while the majority are doing jobs that become less challenging or, indeed, never acquire more than rudimentary capacities necessary to execute simple tasks.

We cannot side with confidence with any one of these views. They are, anyway, as much ideological as based on objective analysis of future skill requirements. The very lack of certainty about future economic and technological developments has thus to be integrated into the premises upon which educational policies (especially those for adult training and retraining) are based. In this context, we single out three desiderata:

   a) The fact that skill requirements, in the economy and for each worker, are rapidly changing implies extensive demands for new learning, retraining provision should be made to meet this;
   b) Computer and technical "literacy" should be interpreted as basic for *everyone* whether or not this knowledge is to be put to immediate use by any given individual;
   c) Economic and technological developments have profound and often disturbing social consequences. This means that the equity goals of recurrent education have actually become more important and that this strategy cannot be narrowly interpreted as one for professional training and retraining alone.

The fundamental question – should recurrent education be geared to preparation for, and adjustment to, working life or should it be an emancipatory strategy to enhance equality of educational and social opportunity? – can therefore be answered simply. *It is, and must be, both.* Viewpoints will differ about priorities and the appropriate balance between these two broad sets of objectives. But debate should cease about which of the two recurrent education should pursue, when they simply are not alternatives. They are indissoluble aspects of education in modern societies whether it be education for the young or for adults. Recurrent education – dubbed the "New Jerusalem" by some (11), a "rising star" by others (12) – not only remains a valid concept, but it has become still more relevant with time.

NOTES AND REFERENCES

1. OECD/CERI (1973), *Recurrent Education: A Strategy for Lifelong Learning*, Paris.
2. See also M. Jourdan (Ed.) (1981), *Recurrent Education in Western Europe – Progress, Projects and Trends in Recurrent, Lifelong and Continuing Education*, NFER – Nelson, Windsor.
3. OECD/CERI (1984), "Towards a Youth Guarantee", Paris (Document on general distribution).
4. It was a prominent item of discussion at the Education Committee Meeting at Ministerial level, 20th-21st November 1984.
5. OECD/CERI (1987), *Adults in Higher Education* (forthcoming), Paris.
6. OECD (1985), *Education and Training after Basic Schooling* (1985), Paris.
7. D. Kallen (1979), "Recurrent Education and Lifelong Learning: Definitions and Distinctions" in T. Schuller and J. McGarry (Eds.). *The World Yearbook of Education: Recurrent Education and Lifelong Learning*, Kogan Page, London and Nicoles, New York.
8. See H.M. Levin and H.G. Schütze (1983), "Economic and Political Dimensions of Recurrent Education", in Levin and Schütze (Eds.), *Financing Recurrent Education – Strategies for Increasing Employment, Job Opportunities, and Productivity*, Sage, Beverly Hills.
9. A. Sorge (1981), "Micro-Electronics and Vocational Education and Training", Berlin (International Management Institute).
10. Office of Technology Assessment (1983), "Automation and the Workplace – Selected Labor, Education and Training Issues", Washington, D.C.
11. M. Blaug and J. Mace (1977), "Recurrent Education: The New Jerusalem?" *Higher Education*, Vol.6, No.3, August.
12. H.M. Levin and H.G. Schütze (1983), "Economic and Political Dimensions of Recurrent Education", *op. cit.*

Chapter II

UNDERSTANDING THE PARTICIPATION OF ADULTS IN EDUCATION IN THE CONTEXT OF CHANGING WORKING AND LIVING PATTERNS

Taking a retrospective view over the last ten years (which is what much of these selected papers attempt), we can see that the concept of recurrent education already has an ontogeny. The biological metaphor is apt because its process of development is not yet complete, because growing things do not always finish up as mere enlargements of their youthful form, and because the core of the matter is organic: recurrent education is nothing if not about, and for, people, however the term comes to be interpreted. This is the point in our enquiry, therefore, where we should begin looking specifically at the human factor with a view to disclosing the range of motives and pressures there are for or against eventual participation in a recurrent education system.

1. Recurrent Education: A Strategic or Descriptive Concept?

Let it be clear at once that in no country does a recurrent education system as yet exist. What has happened, however, is that the original concept, in the course of being examined and developed in the literature and by national or international debate, has become concretised and hence construed in several different ways. The interpretation of recurrent education can differ, however, not only in terms of the concrete components that make it up but also in terms of the nature of the concept.

At least three different uses of "recurrent education" can be distinguished:

   i) Recurrent education can be used very generally as a synonym for lifelong learning and this indeed is probably the most common way the term is used;
   ii) Recurrent education can describe an educational *strategy*, its features and objectives, that aims to realise lifelong learning. This was the sense of the 1973 OECD report (see Chapter I).
   iii) For empirical research into aspects of education or training for adults or for gathering data on existing provision, an operational definition is required that encompasses a certain range of opportunities that one *may* choose to call "recurrent education". There will never be any single "correct" definition in this operational sense. Using a variety of criteria, the researcher or statistical office will, in fact, be addressing the assembly of existing educational provision for adults or a portion of these programmes in a particular country. This usage is relevant here because many of the studies reported in this volume, especially in Chapter III, necessarily are based on such practical, operational concepts.

In (i) and (ii), the definitions are, firstly, *general* and leave unanswered, and deliberately so, precisely what kinds of education and training are consistent with the overall implementation of recurrent education. Secondly, they are *systemic*, i.e. they take their meaning not from any specific arrangements but from the organisation of educational opportunities as a whole, referring to "education" in its broadest sense, and so encompassing also training and non-formal programmes. Hence, they cannot provide a checklist of what "counts" as recurrent education in the here-and-now. Thirdly, they define a broad aim which, if realised, would involve a radical redistribution of educational opportunities, in particular towards a generalised pattern of lifelong learning. These first two definitions differ in terms of whether recurrent education is viewed as an overall descriptive concept or a more specific educational strategy.

The operational third usage of the term, on the other hand, is more concrete, being concerned with actual courses, programmes, and institutions. But it is not necessarily more precise because the definitional task here is one of deciding who and what it is appropriate to include as "recurrent education" or the "recurrent student" – a task that necessarily contains a certain arbitrary element.

These different usages each have problematic aspects and they certainly do not always translate easily one into the other. For operational purposes, for example, it is easy enough to agree that a 65-year-old retired worker or a 35-year-old housewife is an adult, but where should the dividing line in age terms be drawn between "youth" and "adult"? Some might argue that "recurrent education" cannot be reduced simply to mean "education for adults", and hence to ask for a dividing line in age terms is to do violence to the concept. The strategic definition as provided by the original OECD report is meant to encompass *all* post-compulsory education and training albeit reorganised along recurrent lines. Yet, a definition of recurrent education in concrete terms can hardly be simply a description of educational opportunities as they stand now since all OECD countries conform, to a greater or lesser degree, to the "front-end" model. On the other hand, if operational usages exclude the large array of post-compulsory opportunities undertaken straight after school, they invite the risk of recurrent education always being viewed as a fourth sector, attached loosely to the end of the main primary, secondary, and tertiary sectors, and impinging little on them. Furthermore, to exclude those who carry on their studies straight after secondary schooling would seem to contradict one of the fundamental guiding principles – that people should be able to take up education and training throughout their lifetimes *when they choose*. This might mean that they delay further studies after school but it can equally mean that they carry on at least part of their education straight after compulsory schooling if they want to.

Each of these types of definition has its own validity and certainly none enjoy exclusive copyright. Their differences, however, show that care should be taken with usage and that clarity about definitions is just as important now as it was when "recurrent education" first entered the educational lexicon, even if this means reformulation if changed conditions require it. All types are relevant to this volume since the topics covered vary from the general implications of changing living and working patterns for education in the future through to the specific findings about participation in programmes and actual financing mechanisms. All these definitions or usages, however, share the basic principle of lifelong learning – that education should be available to all throughout their lives and not restricted to the early years of childhood and youth.

2. *Two Approaches to the Assessment of Participation and their Limitations*

Since a review of many previous findings is provided in Chapter III, and since the literature on participation in recurrent education is almost as broad as that on recurrent and adult education itself, we will confine ourselves here to general observations about two broad categories of enquiry, showing either (a) a statistical approach or (b) an individual/psychological approach.

a) *The Statistical Approach*

Typified by the use of large-scale surveys, literature in this category has mainly addressed three general and important questions: What is the total number of adult students? Where are they to be found? Who are they? Thus, the approach can provide information on the overall participation rate of adults in a given range of educational settings at a particular time, the numbers in different kinds of courses and institutions, and breakdowns by age, sex, socio-economic status, and previous educational experience. The kinds of education covered in such surveys depend, among other things, upon the institutional arrangements and availability of information in different countries. Rarely are attempts made to consolidate information on adult education, adults in post-compulsory and higher education, and labour market and on-the-job training. These surveys, therefore, span only a certain range of the learning opportunities that might ideally make up a recurrent education system.

For this reason, and because there is no single correct definition either of "adult" or of "education", no precise figure should be expected for the total number or proportion of adults in education during a given period nor, more generally, who might be counted as adult learners. Sometimes enormous lengths are taken to arrive at exact estimates and to try to make comparable quite diverse and arguably incomparable phenomena. The resulting figure, as Cross underlines, can vary from a conservative 11 per cent to a high 98 per cent depending on the definitions used (1). Clearly, measures of such variability are not very meaningful.

Instead of trying to fix with precision something that is necessarily imprecise, more attention could usefully be devoted to constructing categories and definitions most appropriate to each country and most useful to the policy discussion and decision-making process. If it turns out that different sectors and types of education and training are, in reality, incomparable, then it will be only natural that statistics on them are also difficult to compare.

There are genuine problems, therefore, yet not enough to justify the reluctance of many countries to devote greater efforts to gathering regular and comprehensive statistics since not all the problems are, by any means,

insuperable. One of the OECD studies on adult education (2) itemised the major ones as:

i) Uncertainty about the range of activities to be included within the scope of adult education;
ii) Confusion about what is meant by participation;
iii) The existence of a very large number of agencies – some providing learning opportunities for adults as a primary, some as a secondary, function;
iv) A general lack of concern to gather statistics on the part of public authorities and many of the providing agencies;
v) The unreliability of the methods used by agencies to record statistics;
vi) The variety of the methods used to record statistics;
vii) The tendency for a significant percentage of adult learners to participate in more than one educational programme.

Some of these are more serious than others. The greatest stumbling block is, perhaps, the fourth one; that recurrent education and training affects the interests of a large number of the populations of OECD countries and yet there is only lukewarm interest in monitoring it in detail. The other items in the list vary in importance. There is ample room for confusion about the terms "education", "adult", or "participation" but it calls for operational definitions as already discussed. Point (vii) – some participate in more than one course or programme – is simply a reality. For some purposes, the numbers of students will be of interest; for others, the numbers in particular courses. Correspondingly, institutional data can reveal the numbers on a given course or programme while survey data can reveal the actual educational experiences of individuals.

The others in the list are more serious, though again, much depends on the central factor of lack of concern. For, were even a portion of the effort and energy at present devoted to gathering information concerning the traditional school and college sectors channelled into enlarging our understanding of education and training for adults, its diversity and complexity would present a less awesome prospect to the statistician. Nonetheless, it has to be recognised that the number and variety of agencies providing education is a formidable barrier to be broached, not just because their number is large but because of the dispersal of authority under which they are responsible. One question, though, has tended to be exaggerated in importance: how to establish a neat categorisation of the variety of educational experiences and provision that will make for straightforward comparisons? Much of school and college data – in principle, more uniform and easy to classify – cannot be reduced to a simple set of categories. Why, then, should education and training for adults, covering a much more diverse field, be subject to such a demanding constraint?

Despite the need for more statistical information, the value of this data should not be overestimated. Broad-brush descriptive data may enhance knowledge of who the typical adult student is. But they cannot reveal much concerning how social and age-group differences might be redressed nor do they shed much light on atypical adult learners. These may be among the most interesting to analyse. Indeed, there is good reason for mistrust of the lessons often drawn from the statistics. Correlation is, all too easily, assumed to be causation. The dangers of such misinterpretation are especially pronounced in this area with the accompanying risk of drawing erroneous policy lessons.

b) The "Individual/Psychological" Approach

Many studies of participation can be characterised as "individual/psychological". This is because they have focused on the motivations of individuals as the key to understanding why some adults do and others do not participate in education. Second, a principal means of finding out what are the motivations, goals and interests of individuals is to ask them: why, for example, do they or do they not participate in education? What would they study if they were to do so? What do they consider the main obstacles and barriers to their participation?

The main results of studies under this heading are presented in Tables 3 and 4 in Chapter III. Certain other recurring findings might be considered alongside those listed in these Tables. One is that, asked to rank subjects they would be interested in learning, adults often place "vocational" subjects at the top of the list. Yet, whereas the category "vocational" is often not further broken down or differentiated, the other subjects – presumably "non-vocational" – usually are (hobbies, general education, home and family life, or personal development). The prominence given to interest in "vocational" subjects is partly, therefore, a statistical artifact.

Another common finding is that significant differences emerge between what people say they would like to do and what they actually participate in. While such differences are interesting and occur for a complex of reasons, they serve to reduce the weight that should be placed upon any such answers. This suggests that studies of individuals' motivations alone are seriously limited unless combined with those that illuminate the opportunity for, and barriers against, education operative for the same adults. To use Cross' terminology referred to below, the "dispositional" factors should not be studied in isolation.

Perceptions of, and motivations for, learning are significantly dependent upon a number of factors, among which are the very kinds of education available – its visibility, its location, its timing and other related circumstances. Equally, someone who is very occupied – a young parent starting a family, for example, who goes out to work, is paying for a house and car, bringing up young children and trying to maintain a semblance of social life – may well say that he or she is neither very interested, nor has the time or the money, but this is not to say that interest would not be there under different circumstances. A locality where educational opportunities are limited or little visible can generate quite different attitudes among the local community from one where there are flourishing and visible educational facilities and opportunities.

This is not to say that everyone is potentially clamouring at classroom doors, but rather that replies to direct questions about education are alone an unreliable guide to actual interests and behaviour. In any event, should the individual be assumed able to account completely for his or her actions, including future, hypothetical behaviour? Few professional social scientists would make such a bold claim about themselves.

There are, then, limitations on the understanding that can be derived from the kinds of studies referred to here. Going further, some commentators have drawn attention to the social desirability of responses as a major source of bias in the answers people give to surveys and questionnaires of the kind used. In addition, replies to questionnaires and surveys cannot be regarded as constant and final.

Cross (3), in identifying three kinds of barriers to participation – *situational*, *dispositional* and *institutional* – provides a useful framework for accommodating the different factors and approaches considered in this volume:

- "Situational" barriers are those resulting from one's situation in life at a given time; the above-mentioned influences of work, family, social and leisure lives on an adult's participation in education;
- "Dispositional" barriers are related to attitudes and perceptions about oneself as a learner. It is this element which, as we have argued, has been the principal concern of those whose focus falls predominantly within the individual/psychological approach;
- "Institutional" is taken to include those practices and procedures that exclude or discourage working adults from participating in educational activities. This element recognises the crucial influence that supply and provision exert both on how people view education of various kinds, and whether they actually participate or not.

Each of these, extended to include positive factors as well as barriers to participation, is developed in turn in the sections and chapters that follow.

3. Changes in Working Time: Some Implications for Education

Though the availability of time is only one important influence among several upon the participation of adults in education, delineating recent trends in worktime and in the opportunities available in work and leisure can illuminate why some groups typically are more likely than others to take part in various forms of education or training. More generally, developments and trends in work and non-work time, and the related social and economic changes that accompany them, present major challenges for recurrent education to respond to and they will be powerful determinants of the form it will take in the future.

Table 1 shows the broad pattern of changes of annual working hours in a number of OECD countries. The picture is a general one of reduction in average annual working time in these countries. In some, the overall diminution has

Table 1
TRENDS IN AVERAGE ANNUAL HOURS WORKED PER PERSON IN EMPLOYMENT
(a)

1975 = 100

	1975	1976	1977	1978	1979	1980	1981	1982	1983
Canada	100.0	99.5	97.7	98.3	97.7	97.1	96.1	94.7	94.1
Finland	100.0	99.5	99.2	99.3	98.2	97.0	96.7	95.7	94.7
France	100.0	100.2	98.0	97.9	98.2	98.5	97.1	92.7	91.5
Germany	100.0	102.0	100.4	99.0	98.1	97.4	96.6	96.8	96.9
Japan	100.0	101.3	101.4	101.7	102.3	102.0	101.6	101.4	101.5
Italy	100.0	99.9	98.0	97.5	97.2	97.2	96.9	96.5	95.8
Netherlands	100.0	100.5	99.2	96.8	94.4	94.6	95.1	95.6	96.0
Norway	100.0	97.8	95.6	94.4	93.4	93.3	92.1	92.1	91.6
Sweden	100.0	99.1	100.6	98.9	96.4	95.7	94.4	95.3	95.8
United Kingdom	100.0	99.1	98.1	97.0	96.5	94.1	91.1	91.9	91.2
United States	100.0	100.1	100.0	99.7	99.6	98.7	98.4	97.9	98.9

a) These data refer, as far as possible, to the total economy, unless otherwise specified below.

Sources:
Canada: Data supplied by Statistics Canada.
Finland: *Finnish National Accounts* data.
France: Data supplied by Prof. R. Granier, Université de Droit, d'Economie et des Sciences d'Aix-Marseille.
Italy: Provisional data supplied by the Italian authorities (ISTAT).
Germany: Data supplied by the German Institut für Arbeitsmarkt und Berufsforschung.
Japan: Japanese *Yearbook of Labour Statistics*, referring to employees in enterprises with 30 or more employees.
Netherlands: Data supplied by the Netherlands Economisch Instituut voor het Midden- en Kleinbedrijf referring to persons employed in the private enterprise sector excluding agriculture and fishing.
Norway: *Norwegian National Accounts* data.
Sweden: *Swedish National Accounts* data.
United Kingdom: A. Maddison, "Monitoring the Labour Market: A Proposal for a Comprehensive Approach in Official Statistics,,. *Review of Income and Wealth,* June 1980, supplemented by more recent data supplied to the Secretariat by Professor A. Maddison.
United States: 1973–81, *United States National Accounts* data, referring to employees only; 1981–83, unpublished data of the United States Bureau of Labor Statistics, again referring to employees only.

Source: OECD Employment Outlook, 1985, Table J.

been sizeable; in others, rather less significant. On the whole, the 1950s and well into the 1960s were years of stability and sometimes even worktime increase, associated particularly with the post-war reconstruction. It was only the late 1960s and 1970s that saw a quickening general movement towards reduction of worktime.

These patterns are related to structural and sectoral changes. Principal among these are the increasing labour market participation of women (whose hours in the paid labour market are typically shorter than men's), the related growth of part-time work, the often shorter hours of the youngest and oldest members of the workforce, shifts in the occupational structure over recent decades, and the related changes in the size of the different economic sectors. These structural factors are important sources of worktime reduction even if they carry different implications from the secular reduction of contracted weekly or annual hours of given workers.

Some groups thus work longer hours on the whole than others. Manual workers often put in extensive hours as do higher-level professionals and managers. In between, middle-level white-collar workers tend to work a shorter week with less overtime and often with more substantial annual holidays than manual workers. Sex and status differences in working hours are not unrelated since many white-collar and clerical jobs are held by women. Working hours systematically vary not only on the basis of social, sex and age grouping but by economic sector, industry, and type of firm as well. Agriculture, for example, is typically associated with very long hours whereas services can entail below-average worktime.

As pertinent a source of worktime changes as those for the year are those for the whole lifespan, which have perhaps more far-reaching consequences for recurrent education. Whether lifetime working has on average risen or fallen depends on whether it is viewed in absolute or in relative terms. In absolute terms, over the last several decades the total number of years that comprise working careers tend to be longer than they were because of greater longevity, while the increased participation of women in work outside the home has actually meant that more people now spend substantial parts of their lives working in the paid labour market. In relative terms, however, the ratio of working life to the total lifespan has shifted in the opposite direction due largely to three main factors: the increased longevity and hence retirement phase, the more extensive periods spent in education before entering the labour market, and the tendency for retirement and partial or total withdrawal from the labour market to come earlier in life. As work becomes a less dominating activity timewise in people's lives, the potential for education to play a more important role may be a substantial one.

Certain group differences within the global averages are interesting. Women live significantly longer than men and the gap has been growing. In several countries, the average difference in life expectancy is about 5 or 6 years, with the resultant alteration of the profile of the oldest members of the population. Another qualification to the main pattern is that social group differences remain sizeable and, despite improvements in health and health care, the less privileged sections of the population are still much more likely to have only a short retirement compared with their more advantaged contemporaries.

This is, of course, only the briefest sketch of what in reality is a highly complex set of patterns and trends. These trends are certainly relevant to the issue of adult participation in education. One of their implications is that people have more time that potentially can be used for education. Care, of course, must be taken with this kind of conclusion – reduction in worktime in the paid labour market does not necessarily imply free time for everyone in the labour force (mothers who go out to work being a good example). Nevertheless, the availability of time is one of the most important enabling or constraining factors vis-à-vis a return to education.

It is the form in which work and non-worktime is changing that is, perhaps, of greater significance. Work-week reductions may have only limited significance for education compared with annual and career worktime changes. That is, when education is placed beside all the other activities of people's lives, an hour or two more free time in the week may not greatly change education's attractiveness. This is likely to be especially true for those whose gains over recent years have been accompanied by greater intensity at work or a counter-balancing increase in the journey to and from the workplace. More extensive vacations and holidays, as opposed to weekly worktime reductions probably carry rather different implications. Vacations frequently involve travel and an opening of new horizons, which for many will have a real, if often intangible, effect upon the desire to learn. Vacations also provide a substantial period away from work so that new and different activities can be undertaken in a way that the extra hour or two in the week does not allow. The importance of these effects again should not be exaggerated. For many people, extra vacation entitlements will be taken as longer holidays not in summer schools or residential courses. The potential, nonetheless, is there, and many already use some of their vacation for organised learning and courses that otherwise they would not have had enough time for.

The *work-life* changes carry, perhaps, the most far-reaching implications for recurrent education. As work becomes increasingly compressed into the middle period of people's lives, one of its results has been the creation of older citizens outside the labour market in much larger numbers than before. The challenges this poses have scarcely begun to be met, but as they are, education should become a major activity for older people. More generally, the altered balance of work to other activities over the life cycle also raises the prospect of other activities and occupations becoming personally and socially elevated to a level comparable to that now enjoyed exclusively by work. Definitions of self and of socially useful activity, which have been dominated by this one criterion, should come increasingly to find a place for others. And education should be foremost among them.

These trends raise the further question of whether it is personally, economically, or socially desirable that work should become increasingly exclusive to those in the middle years of their lives, leaving the basic pattern of education-work-retirement unchanged? Do the younger and older members of the population want to be increasingly excluded from work and should they be? Do those in the middle years of their life want work to be their predominant occupation?

Recurrent education, as the alternation between education, work, and the other main life activities, clearly lies at the heart of these questions.

Worktime could well continue to fall, even markedly, over the next decade or two. But it might imply financial sacrifices by those workers with jobs that not all, at present, show themselves willing to undergo (4). Yet some analyses suggest that a marked gain in non-worktime could be experienced over the next fifteen years or so at no significant financial cost to individuals (5).

If there is, as suggested here, a changing mixture of work and non-work time, then education and training should be re-organised as part of this change. Recurrent education, with its dual emphasis upon breaking into the overly rigid education-work-retirement sequence and upon facilitating the alternation of education with other activities, is a prime candidate as an organising strategy for education and training in such a context. Yet, while an attractive and important potential for recurrent education can be painted in general terms, how do the arguments survive confrontation with the "real world", typified as it is by problems and constraints and not just attractive ambitions for education? It is to this that we now turn.

4. Other Changes in Work and Leisure

Changes in the Labour Market

When the labour market is discussed in relation to recurrent education, the issues raised have often been treated as if they concerned only regular, day-time, full-time jobs in the formal sector, usually in industry. This certainly facilitates the delineation of such factors as the respective responsibilities for training provision and finance among the industrial partners, and for educational benefits such as paid educational leave of absence; yet it is an image that is increasingly partial and unrepresentative. Rather, part-time work, shift schedules, temporary work, casual and black labour markets are growing. By examining these developments, the possibilities for participating in recurrent education for certain adults, especially those who are disadvantaged, become clearer. And such examination warns that the road to the realisation of recurrent education is far from a simple one.

Part-time work has been growing steadily, associated with the increased participation of women in the labour market, though it differs considerably in importance from country to country (see *Table 2*). By 1983, a fifth of all employment in OECD countries was part-time, two-thirds of which accounted for by women. What is not clear from these figures is how many of those who work part-time do so out of choice in order to meet other demands in their lives and how many accept it involuntarily, faced with very few openings in the market of full-time jobs (6). The groups who predominate in part-time work are often regarded as, in some way, marginal workers – women with housekeeping and child-rearing responsibilities, students, semi-retired workers. Such employment

Table 2
THE SIZE COMPOSITION OF PART-TIME EMPLOYMENT, 1973-83

Percentages

	Part-time employment as a proportion of						Women's share in Part-time Employment	
	Total Employment		Male Employment		Female Employment			
	1973	1983 (a)	1973	1983 (a)	1973	1983 (a)	1973	1983 (a)
Australia	11.4	17.2	3.4	6.1	27.3	35.9	79.6	77.8
Austria	6.4	8.3	1.4	1.5	15.6	19.8	85.8	88.4
Belgium	3.8	8.1	1.0	2.0	10.2	19.7	82.3	84.0
Canada	10.6 (b)	15.4	5.1 (b)	7.6	20.3 (b)	26.2	69.5 (b)	71.3
Denmark	21.2 (b)	23.7	4.7 (b)	6.6	45.1 (b)	44.7	86.8 (b)	84.7
Finland	6.7 (c)	8.3	3.3 (c)	4.5	10.5 (c)	12.5	72.8 (c)	72.1
France	7.2	9.7	2.6	2.6	14.7	20.1	77.9	84.6
Germany	10.1	12.6	1.8	1.7	24.4	30.0	89.0	91.9
Greece	–	6.5	–	3.7	–	12.1	–	61.2
Ireland	6.7 (b)	6.7	2.7 (b)	2.7	16.8 (b)	15.7	71.4 (b)	72.0
Italy	6.4	4.6	3.7	2.4	14.0	9.4	58.3	64.8
Japan	7.9	10.5	4.6	4.8	14.7	21.1	60.9	70.7
Luxembourg	6.7	6.9	1.0	1.0	18.4	18.8	77.8	90.0
Netherlands (d)	8.7	21.2	2.4	6.9	26.2	50.3	80.2	78.4
New Zealand	10.8	14.6	4.7	5.2	22.0	28.3	71.3	79.0
Norway	23.5 (b)	30.0	8.7 (b)	11.7	47.6 (b)	54.8	77.0 (b)	77.3
Sweden	18.0	25.4	3.7	7.3	38.8	46.2	88.0	84.6
United Kingdom	16.0	19.1	2.3	3.3	39.1	42.4	90.9	89.6
United States (e)	14.0	14.4	7.2	7.6	23.8	23.3	68.4	70.3
	(16.6)	(20.0)	(9.4)	(12.5)	(27.9)	(29.4)	(65.5)	(65.0)

a) The number of non-declared persons in the 1983 data for the EEC countries is distributed proportionately between full-time and part-time employment.
b) 1975
c) 1976
d) Data for 1983 are not comparable with earlier years because of a change in the definition of part-time workers. For details see Note A of the Technical Annex.
e) Part-time workers for economic reasons are excluded from both part-time and total employment. Data in parentheses show the results of including this group in the calculations.

Source: OECD Employment Outlook, 1985, Table 10.

frequently entails lack of job security, less than full social insurance and pension rights, and few benefits generally; it appears, too, that the hourly earnings of part-time manual workers are on average lower than those on full-time schedules (7). Much of part-time work is available in routine jobs so this trend can be seen as part of the expansion of the secondary labour market.

In relation to recurrent education, the implications are complex. For some, part-time work can represent a greater freedom from work to pursue other activities, among which can be education. In this sense, it is deliberate and chosen in order to allow greater personal flexibility and to develop other interests. It is unlikely, however, that this is typical although more might be expected to opt for part-time work for this reason in the future. On the other hand, because the jobs are often routine and associated with low security and fewer benefits, most of this sizeable minority of the workforce is excluded from training which forms part of a pattern of career development, and sometimes from rights to educational leave of absence. Proposals to extend educational leave of absence must take account of the fact, therefore, that a growing proportion of employees is beyond its reach.

In terms of the causes for its expansion, part-time work can be associated with another phenomenon which is taking on significant proportions in some OECD countries – *temporary work*. Employers seek greater flexibility and this may well involve by-passing the extensive and expensive rights of protection that full-time workers have gained over the years. Temporary work often displays even more of the secondary labour market characteristics than does part-time work. While as a proportion of the labour force it may still not be large, in terms of absolute numbers and growth rates, temporary work is certainly a significant development and could well grow still more in the future unless unemployment levels were to fall or non-wage labour costs to decline – neither of which is likely at present.

Casual and black market work are, for obvious reasons, much more difficult to get precise information on. A cautious estimate suggests that in most OECD countries the "hidden economy" amounts to approximately 4 per cent of GDP (8). Estimates by others range from around 10 to as much as 25 per cent in some countries.

Again, making sense of this for recurrent education is not simple. Whether the aim is to break into the education-work-retirement life pattern to promote recurrent education, or whether it is to introduce greater coherence into educational provision so that the labour force possesses a higher level of skills and flexibility, the growth of this "fringe" employment limits the relevance of such educational provision to a decreasing section of the work force. Members of the fringe (part-time, temporary, casual, undeclared workers) are, of course, largely outside the legislative measures that extend rights, including rights to education, to workers; outside conventional bargaining structures where education is an important item on the agenda; outside structures that would allow the individual a view of his or her career as a whole and the role education and training can play in it.

The phenomenon of shift-work is another development of interest to the question of participation in recurrent education. By 1978, an ILO report suggested that shiftworkers accounted for some 20 per cent or more of the work force in several of the OECD countries, increasingly extending to groups who before were rarely touched by work-scheduling of this kind, and this proportion may well have risen since (9). At one time, it was largely restricted to certain traditional manual occupational sectors such as mining, steel, and railway workers but more and more services and offices are now adopting shift systems and women more frequently work on such schedules. So, while the assumption is often made that people work a "normal" day and keep regular and social hours, this is no longer true for a sizeable minority of the work force.

As far as education is concerned, these workers are typified by schedules which make them unavailable during hours when education provision is most likely to be available and, if they are on rotating shifts, by the continual changing of the times when they are free from work. Moreover, there are so many variations in shift schedules that no simple formula to make recurrent education more feasible would affect more than pockets of shift workers. And social groups that have repeatedly shown up in recurrent education studies as low participators are high among those who work shifts (such as semi- and unskilled manual workers, immigrants and migrants, older if not the oldest members of the work force). Given that this form of working is disruptive of activities that others are able to follow, given that groups who are unlikely to participate in recurrent education are numerous among shiftworkers, and given that a sizeable proportion of the workforce are working shifts, explicit attention should be given to the question of how education can best be made available to them. Some, such as those on permanent morning or evening shifts, may be able to follow courses in their own time during the day. But for many of the rest, it would most likely have to be made available at the workplace, during working hours, or else be taken in the form of extended leave of absence if a significant increase in educational participation is to occur.

Although it is impossible here adequately to cover the range of questions and issues arising from the increased participation of women in the workforce, a discussion of changes in the labour market can hardly omit such a fundamental development (10). Across OECD countries, the traditional ethic of women, especially married women, staying at home has been disappearing and while men's participation in the labour force has decreased, women's has steadily risen. Yet, the notion of a continuing career for women is still not possible in many cases, especially as they are so highly concentrated in certain occupations doing largely feminised jobs. Nor does there appear to be much change in the occupational segregation of women, even though they now make up such a sizeable proportion of the workforce (11). This clearly has considerable effect on the opportunities for, and participation of, women in that education which is closely related to work – in terms of the sorts of education and training made available, and in terms of career openings.

It is also clear that education and training for women who have been out of the labour force for a significant period of time is one of the principal means of allowing them to re-enter and re-integrate into the labour market. Recurrent education is also vital in the equalisation of their position in the workplace, both in terms of creating more job opportunities for women and in terms of breaking down the concentration in feminised occupations. Yet, considerably more than occupational training and vocational education is required for this equality to be achieved. The traditional sex roles are extremely resilient and many women hold a paid job while continuing to be largely responsible for the unremunerated household and child-rearing tasks. Working women have significantly less spare time, on average, than either working men or other groups of women. In terms of time, therefore, paid work may represent as much of a barrier to participation in recurrent education as it does "liberation" from the household, a factor which should not be forgotten in ensuring that women are able to profit fully from educational opportunities.

Leisure and Out-of-Work Life

"Leisure" is a difficult concept that eludes precise definition. One way that it has been studied is through the time-budget approach. The findings they reveal are relevant to the question of attracting more adult students, for there are some indications that, while people on average have more spare time and are working less, much of this spare time is taken up with passive, relaxing pursuits rather than active, demanding ones. Some have suggested that we are entering the post-industrious society as well as the post-industrial one. It is to be expected, therefore, that relatively modest increases in non-work time will not necessarily have significant consequences for participation in education – insofar as education is an active and demanding pursuit.

The time-budget data also show the importance now of individualistic lifestyles centred upon the home with an increasingly distant relationship from the immediate community. This has different, even somewhat contradictory, implications for education. Private lifestyles may prove in conflict with the public nature of education yet some people may increasingly be drawn to modes of learning which take place in the home, rather than attend a specific institution. A more far-reaching implication for education may be that it is increasingly required to provide focal points for communities that are losing their other traditional institutions. It is well known that many adult students seek social contact as well as knowledge when they enrol in education.

Understanding how best to make education available to adults can thus be enhanced through attention to dominant features of the working and out-of-work lives of specific groups. To focus on one group only that we have mentioned already – shiftworkers – those who manage to adapt to this way of scheduling their lives often do so by altering entirely their lifestyles to meet the changing and unsocial hours. This may well include the pursuit of solitary occupations that require no special times when they need be undertaken. For this group, individualised, distance learning could well be effective and an untapped source of adult demand for learning opportunities might be met through innovative applications of new educational technology. Similarly for other identifiable sections of the population, attention to the overall features and effects of their working and out-of-working lives will clarify the possibilities for them to return to education.

A common theme in the study of leisure has been the close relationship that exists between working and out-of-work lives and, in particular, the effects on leisure and spare-time pursuits of holding an unrewarding, routine job. With monotonous jobs, there is the tendency for people to look either for relaxing pursuits or else "explosive" activities in order to dissipate the tensions of unsatisfactory working environments. It is unsurprising in the light of this that efforts to increase the participation of under-represented groups in recurrent education often meet with only limited success. The effects of work go well beyond the workplace – "the long arm of the job", as it has been aptly called.

5. Some Conclusions

In reviewing the trends and phenomena addressed in this chapter, the picture for recurrent education is both discouraging and promising.

The difficulties for the realisation of recurrent education are not to be underestimated, as Chapter I underlines. The very economic and social changes that argue for greater flexibility often reinforce inflexibility, not the reverse. It is little surprising that those occupying secure jobs with visible career structures become reluctant to step out for educational purposes unless they are sure their job is guaranteed. Existing patterns of participation in adult education tend to reinforce educational inequalities, not reduce them. The education-work-retirement sequence has, in some respects, become more deeply entrenched in the last decade, not less as some were predicting when recurrent education was first developed. Segmentation and barriers to entry in the labour market also appear to have become more pronounced in many countries thereby placing severe limits on the immediate role education and training can play for the labour market advancement of certain groups. Equally, developments in the labour market (including a growing "marginalisation"), place many adults outside the structures and institutions that have traditionally been viewed as the settings through which a recurrent education strategy could best be realised.

The promise of recurrent education remains, however, a compelling one. As a new mixture of work and non-work emerges (and this includes growing and high levels of unemployment), greater participation in education and a reorganisation of the overly rigid education-work-retirement sequence are both desirable and necessary. The widespread agreement on the need for a flexible and skilled workforce, capable of adapting to changing needs as knowledge rapidly becomes obsolete, argues forcefully too in favour of the reorganisation of education and training. The argument that the present waste of resources and potential that unemployment represents should be spent in ways either useful to the individual or to society or, better still, to both together, is hard to fault and recurrent education offers the basis on which this can be realised.

To this can be added the need for education throughout the life-cycle to be seen as itself an integral component of life-chances rather than purely as a selective mechanism for life-chances defined in labour market terms. That is, an egalitarian educational policy based on the latter is bound to meet with disappointment when there are not enough jobs, let alone desirable jobs, for all that want them. Education for the multitude of roles and purposes beyond that of preparation and selection for work – roles that are social, political, cultural, and private – should thus make up an important component of life-chances in the future. This is surely a challenge that requires the reorganisation of education along recurrent lines.

NOTES AND REFERENCES

1. K.P. Cross (1979), "Adult Learners: Characteristics, Needs and Interests" in Peterson R.E. & Associates (Eds.) *Lifelong Learning in America*, Jossey-Bass, San Francisco, Washington, London.
2. OECD (1977) *Learning Opportunities for Adults*, Vol. IV, *Participation in Adult Education*, Paris.
3. K.P. Cross (1979), *op cit.*
4. See OECD (1982), *Labour Supply, Growth Constraints and Work-Sharing*, Paris.
5. Fred Best (1981), *Work-Sharing: Issues, Policy Options and Prospects*, The W.E. Upjohn Institute for Employment Research, Kalamazoo, pp. 139-140.
6. The evidence from four countries seems to suggest that the majority of part-time workers are voluntary, see *OECD Employment Outlook*, Paris, 1983, Chapter IV.
7. See OECD *Employment Outlook* 1983, p. 51.
8. Derek Blades (1982), "The Hidden Economy and National Accounts", in *OECD Observer No. 114* (January), pp. 15-17.
9. ILO (1978), *The Management of Working Time*, Geneva. See also the Country Studies on the Spread of Shiftwork for the European Foundation fo the Improvement of Living and Working Conditions, Dublin.
10. Liba Paukert (1984), *The Employment and Unemployment of Women in OECD Countries*, OECD, Paris.
11. OECD (1985), *The Integration of Women into the Economy*, Paris, Chapter II.

Chapter III
PARTICIPATION IN RECURRENT EDUCATION: A RESEARCH REVIEW

1. Starting Point and Purpose

The educational optimism of the fifties and sixties no longer exists and instead there has been a growing scepticism about education. The expansion which took place in the educational sector during the 1960s has not resulted in the expected increase in equality and economic growth. Growing criticism of existing education systems has led to increasing interest in the idea of recurrent education. Unless special measures are taken to support underprivileged groups, however, an expanded system of recurrent education is very likely to increase the differences within and between generations. Experience derived from the experiments that have been conducted so far points to no major progress in this direction. (See OECD, 1975, Cross, 1979; Kim, 1979; Abrahamsson and Rubenson, 1981). For instance, open universities which have been tried in various forms have mainly attracted a group that has already been relatively favoured educationally (Tunstall, 1974).

The right to educational leave is a fundamental prerequisite in the development of a system of recurrent education. This right has already been established in many OECD countries, either by law or by virtue of collective bargaining. It is too early yet to comment on the effects of this reform, but the available information suggests that women and the educationally underprivileged make the least use of this right (OECD/CERI, 1976; OECD/CERI, 1978).

To correct the social bias of recruitment, a system of recurrent education needs to include positive discrimination in favour of the educationally weakest groups. In addition to socio-economic measures, greater interest will have to be devoted to the total living situation of these people. Participation by adults in education beyond the compulsory level is not an activity apart from the rest of a person's life; it is closely bound up with various adult roles – vocational, social, family, and leisure. So, if we are to take the right steps to realise the idea of recurrent education, we must improve our understanding of why adults participate in education and the factors that influence their motivation.

Research so far into recruitment and motivation unfortunately lacks both theoretical application and an overall view. This has inhibited the development of research and limited the possibilities of taking practical measures in the light of existing findings. The report that now follows must be seen against this background.

As Mezirow (1971) and Boshier (1973) have observed, research into recruitment of adults has been inhibited by lack of interest in formulating a testable theory. Studies have been mainly concerned with describing who takes part in adult education, classified in terms of background factors such as age, education, and social status. With the exception of a few isolated instances (e.g. Lehtonen and Tuomisto, 1974; Boshier, 1973; Rubenson, 1975; Cross, 1981), a theoretical approach and an attempt to construct a model are lacking. Researchers have generally been content to describe their own findings without relating them to the findings that have emerged from comparable investigations. Research so far has tended neither to yield new points of inquiry nor to confirm uncertain findings nor develop new methods.

What is more, an applicable theory is lacking not only as regards participation in education but also concerning social participation generally (McClosky, quoted in Boshier, 1973; Dumazedier, 1974). Where there has been a discussion concerning the level at which a theory should exist, the conclusion seems to be that it is impossible to explain such complex events as participation in adult education on the basis of a single, comprehensive theory.

According to McClosky (quoted in Boshier, 1973), all that one can hope to do is to "group the relative independent variables into those influences essentially internal (psychological and cognitive) and those derived from the individual's external environment". Miller (1967) argues on similar lines, but he goes one step further when he maintains that:

> We can do little more at this point than sketch in some hypothesised relations among the variables which appear to have some bearing on the appearance in our programmes of some adults rather than others, in some programmes rather than others, at particular times rather than others. Without such a guide we are condemned for ever to repeating status surveys and refining our empirical categories to the point of meaninglessness.

Introducing an analysis of the sociology of leisure, in which adult education is one of the subsidiary aspects considered, Dumazedier (1974) writes:

> The time is not yet ripe to devise a sociological theory of leisure, despite the interest afforded by attempts of theorising. However, in this complex and troubled time in which certainties are questioned everywhere, analysing the endeavours and the findings of empirical sociology appears to be the most useful way of liberating theoretical thought from the delusions of dogmatism and of guiding practical action away from the powerlessness of mere practicality. Yet, whatever its limitations, factual data provides landmarks without which sociological analysis – whether concerned with practical change or with the progress of theory – will reduce to mere speculation.

The current standpoint therefore seems to be that one cannot hope to arrive at an over-riding theory explaining adult participation in education; instead one should describe the inter-relatedness of different groups of variables on the basis of empirical research.

Considering the studies which have appeared so far in adult education, it is doubtful whether they can provide the basis for a fruitful synthesis of knowledge, in the sense of attaining a higher intradisciplinary level of understanding. Existing attempts at theoretical structures have been criticised for focusing too much on the individual (Lehtonen and Tuomisto, 1974; Knudsen and Skaalvik, 1979). It is almost as though all problems concerning recruitment could be reduced to psychological ones. (This point is discussed in more detail in the previous chapter.) However, only having a point of departure on the macro level (e.g. the social class factor) would be to deny the differences which have been demonstrated within different social strata. Thus analysis of recruitment has to consider both the macro and the micro levels, i.e. both structural conditions and individual psychological factors and, in addition, the link between them.

If participation in adult education is taken as a "territory" for research (see Törnebom, 1974), the knowledge hitherto gained resembles patches on the map. Without at least some idea of the contours on the map, however, it will be impossible to plot the experience we gain, ignorant as we are of the relations between the parts. An over-riding structure, even if its quality is deficient, could serve as a rough master sketch, thereby furnishing a basis for a synthesis of the scattered knowledge available. It is in order to develop such a framework for understanding the results of isolated studies of participation and recruitment that this chapter presents a model or paradigm which is intended to provide, in the words of Gage (1963), "... ways of thinking or patterns for research that, when carried out, can lead to the development of theory." As a background to the model, the next section examines general theories of motivation, linking the individual's decision regarding participation with the prevailing structural and cultural conditions in society.

2. Theories of Motivation

A review of psychology textbooks will show that there are several serious theoretical approaches (see Koch, 1959; Cofer and Appley, 1964; Madsen, 1968; Korman, 1974.) As the textbooks show, these approaches can be grouped in various ways. Korman (1974) distinguishes three schools. The first – drive theories – are rooted in biology and physics, and draw on a physiological research tradition. This school emerged at the close of the 19th century, and was profoundly influenced by the scientific tradition represented by the doctrines of Darwin. Watson, Hull, Spence, and Brown are among the exponents of this approach. They use terms such as drives and instincts to explain the origin, control, and persistence of behaviour. Behaviour is described in terms of stimulus-response chains.

A second school starts with such concepts as emotions, needs, and motives. Human behaviour is explained in terms of acquired experience and the psychological environment in which the individual finds himself placed. Cognitive processes are taken into consideration, albeit superficially in many cases. Lewin,

Tolman, McClelland, Atkinson, and Vroom are prominent exponents of this approach, which we shall term "cognitive".

Finally, Korman refers to a philosophical and theological tradition which dominated the sector until our own century, and which has been revived in humanist psychology. Self-realisation is one of the fundamental concepts of this approach. According to the theory of self-realisation, man possesses an innate ability and urge to lead a rich and meaningful life but has been prevented from doing so by factors in his environment. One of the ardent supporters of this view is Maslow, who has developed a theory in which needs are regarded as being hierarchically organised.

It has been argued elsewhere (Rubenson, 1976) that the cognitive school provides a more fruitful starting point than either the humanist or the scientific-physical approaches. Whereas Maslow's humanist approach is virtually devoid of empirical support and the drive theories have proved to be seriously limited, the cognitive direction, despite certain limitations, has proved a valuable aid to the explanation of complex behaviour. It starts with an organic world picture. Exponents have not been content with studying animals or human behaviour in a laboratory situation but have also taken an interest in behaviour occurring in real life. This is particularly true of the specific branch of cognitive approaches usually referred to as the *expectancy-valence* theory, which I believe can have a stimulating and elucidating effect on recruitment research and also on the design and direction of recurrent education.

Vroom (1964) has given what is, perhaps, the most explicit formulation of an expectancy-valence model and the clearest definition of the meaning of the concept. (For a more detailed description of the theory, see Atkinson and Raynor, 1974.) As Vroom defines it, "valence" expresses an affective attitude to the result of an action; it does not measure a person's attitude to activity *per se*, but is concerned primarily with what the activity can lead to in the future. The measurement of valence ranges from positive (+1) if a person has a strong preference for attaining the expected results, neutral if indifferent to it, and negative (-1) if the individual strongly prefers not to attain it. This concept is, therefore, associated with an individual's attitude towards the results of an action and is quite distinct from the concept of value, which is concerned with the actual satisfaction derived from the action itself.

This is not to deny that an activity can possess intrinsic value. As Houle (1961) found, there are many people who participate in adult education for the sake of the studies themselves. However, our model follows Vroom in concentrating on an individual's expectations about the future results or outcome of an activity (expectancy), and the strength of his preference for the expected outcome (valence). These together exert a force that determines whether an individual is likely to participate in an activity. Figure 1 shows how this theory can be applied to recruitment in adult education.

Figure 1
THE EXPECTANCY-VALENCE THEORY APPLIED TO RECRUITMENT IN ADULT EDUCATION

Sees participation in adult education
as a conceivable means of satisfying
perceived needs (valence)

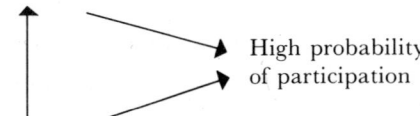

High probability of participation

Believes that he or she is in a position
to complete and successfully cope with
a course, and believes that participation
will have certain desirable consequences
(expectancy)

3. An Analysis of Valence and Expectancy in Terms of Adult Education

Motives for Study and Recruitment Obstacles

No previous study has attempted to relate the valence and expectancy factors directly to participation in adult education. Instead most studies deal with such aspects as motives for study, recruitment obstacles, and "who participates". The following sections summarise the results of such studies.

Far more interest has been devoted to motives for study than to recruitment impediments, but to understand recruitment patterns, it is necessary to take account of both obstacles and motives. Unfortunately, obstacles to recruitment have often been identified in the external environment, and less attention has been paid to psychological impediments – impediments deriving from the self-confidence of the individual, levels of aspiration, and attitudes to adult education. This may give the impression that most people not participating in adult education are highly motivated, but prevented by external factors from taking advantage of opportunities provided. This obscures that the explanation may lie in such obstacles as "lack of interest in education", or "can spend the time in other ways".

Table 3 summarises available evidence on motivation, while Table 4 some of the limited evidence on obstacles to study. It suggests that the most powerful psychological impediment to participation in adult education is the individual's belief that it would not improve his or her general living situation or position on the labour market. Education is regarded as "not my cup of tea". In many, though by no means all cases, this is connected with a negative experience of school (Rubenson, 1975).

Table 3
ADULTS' MOTIVES FOR PARTICIPATION IN EDUCATION

Findings	Authors
One powerful reason for participating is the desire to make practical use of the knowledge acquired.	Taugh (1969), Johnstone & Rivera (1965) Robinson (1970), NIAE (1972), Cross (1981), Karl, (1979)
Lower social class individuals, who have relatively simple jobs, mostly state that they participated in order to be able to change jobs, while those of intermediate and high status, who have jobs presenting opportunities for social development, mostly state "a help in my present job."	Johnstone & Rivera (1965) Kamienski (1975) Johansson & Ekerwald (1976)
The difference between younger and older persons regarding the "for my own work" motive is more pronounced among under-educated persons than among those who had prolonged schooling.	L.O. (1968) Johnstone & Rivera (1965)
Non-vocational motives, such as improving one's general knowledge and having something enjoyable to do in one's spare time, are far more common among persons of intermediate or high social status than among persons of low social status.	London et al. (1963) Douglas & Moss (1968) Cross (1979)
Housewives are more likely to state that they participate to "get out of the rut" and "see new faces".	Emanuelsson et al. (1973) Johnstone & Rivera (1965) Rubenson et al. (1976)
Hobby-oriented courses play an important part in providing opportunities of social contact for persons whose situation otherwise presents limited opportunites of this kind, e.g. housewives.	Rubenson et al. (1976)
In contrast to the younger age categories, the "61 and over" group present no significant differences in motives between the sexes.	Johnsson (1973)
Pensioners look for courses where they can acquire knowledge which will help them to adjust to their new role in society. This demand is far greater than the supply of such courses would suggest.	Hiemstra (1972)
"Preparation for a new job" is mainly emphasized by persons under 30 and by women in the process of changing from child care to gainful employment.	Emanuelson et al. (19730 Johnstone & Rivera (1965)
Most of the persons taking part in adult studies leading to particular qualifications are not doing so because they had long considered beginning to study but because they are in a situation which required them to study (a change of family situation, illness, a change of work, etc.).	Johansson & Ekerwald (1976)

Table 4
IMPEDIMENTS TO RECRUITMENT

Findings	Authors
Persons who are interested in participating are less likely to plead psychological impediments than those who are uninterested, while external obstacles are quoted by both groups to the same extent.	Johnstone & Rivera (1965)
Those who had participated in education seldom referred to such impediments as "had enough of school" and "got enough out of life without participating", while those who had neither participated nor desired to do so are characterised by their reference to these impediments.	Rubenson (1975)
Persons who are interested but have never actually participated tend more than others to state "lack of information".	Rubenson (1975)
Fear of studies is greater among older persons than among younger ones.	London et al. (1963) Molander (1973) Cross (1979)
No age differences between under-educated regarding "lack of time" and "lack of information". On the other hand, fear of studies increases with rising age, as does the feeling that there is no point in studying.	Rubenson et al. (1976) Cross (1981)
Women are more likely than men to cite the cost of education as a barrier.	Cross (1981)
Psychological impediments such as "not certain of being able to cope with education" are related to the anxiety which the individual felt in the school situation in grade 6 of elementary school (13 years of age).	Rubenson (1975)
Lack of economic support is a major barrier to full-time study.	Rubenson et al. (1976) Johansson & Ekerwald (1976) Cross (1981)

This emphasis on psychological impediments does not deny the importance of obstacles in the external environment. As transpired from the experimental activities in Sweden run by the Committee on Methods Testing in Adult Education (SOU 1974), the availability of courses entirely or in part during working hours has a powerful and positive recruitment effect. Thus three-quarters of the shift-workers who were offered the chance to study in working hours felt that the conditions attached to studies directly influenced their decision to participate. On the other hand the incentive grant of Skr. 300 had no perceptible effect. Study assistance in the form of compensation for the extra expenditure involved on fares, meals, and child care had a certain effect on recruitment among housewives but was otherwise immaterial. So, if we are to understand recruitment problems, we have to observe both external environmental and internal psychological obstacles.

Who Takes Part in Adult Education?

Results of research on this aspect of the problem are summarised in Table 5. They confirm the conclusions of the previous two tables. According to the theories of motivation illustrated in Figure 1, participation is very much dependent on whether the individual sees any future value in education. The findings presented in Tables 3 to 5 lend a certain measure of support to this. One reason for the relatively low participation of the under-educated and for the declining educational interest of persons over 40 may well be an incongruency between the demands made on people and the educational opportunities available to them. In addition, where relevant opportunities do exist, people may nonetheless be incapable of relating their current needs to those opportunities.

Self-Evaluation

We suggested, as expressed in Figure 1, that a person's expectancy concerning studies can influence participation, either directly or indirectly via the connection between expectancy and valence. The self-evaluation of the individual is an important factor. Several theories, including Heider's (1958) theory of equilibrium and Festinger's (1957) theory of dissonance suggest that people are motivated to seek states compatible with the views they have acquired concerning themselves, others, and the world around them. An incongruent world (i.e. one that does not agree with one's own world picture) is believed by these writers to evoke anxiety (see Rogers, 1959) so that people try to ensure that their actual situation can be reconciled with their pre-existing world picture.

The individual's view of other people and of the surrounding world is centrally related to the view he takes of himself. Values inconsistent with the individual's evaluation of himself are likely to be rejected. Lecky (1945) argues that the individual sees the world from his own viewpoint, with himself at the centre. Any value entering the system which is inconsistent with the individual's evaluation of himself cannot be assimilated; it meets with resistance and is likely, unless a general reorganisation occurs, to be rejected.

Sjöstrand (1974) defined self-evaluation as the general or global value that the individual ascribes to himself as an object, and he related attitudes and evaluation as follows:

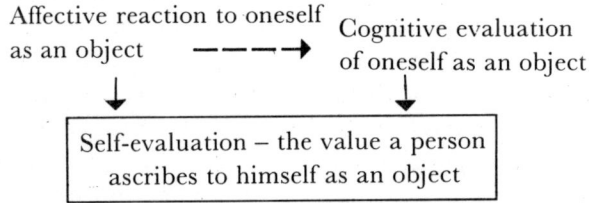

Table 5
RESULTS OF STUDIES COMPARING PARTICIPANTS AND NON-PARTICIPANTS

Findings	Authors
Parental social status is connected with participation.	Husén (1969), Knox (1970), Johnstone & Rivera (1965)
There is a connection between the interest taken by parents in their children's schooling and the extent to which the children later participate in adult education.	Johnstone & Rivera (1965) Rubenson (1972, 1975) Molander (1973), Olofsson (1981)
There is a connection between formal education and participation.	Johnstone & Rivera (1965) Molander (1973), Rubenson (1975) Cross (1979), Kim (1979)
The individual's attitude to his/her own school career (1) has already helped determine educational level at school. No connection with attitude is found, therefore, when the educational level is controlled.	Parker & Paisley (1966) London (1970), Knoz (1970) Rubenson (1975)
There are no great differences between men and woman as regards total participation. The differences are in type of participation.	The LO member .... (1968) Johnstone & Rivera (1965) Cross (1979)
There is a positive correlation between the desire to change occupations and interest in adult education	Rubenson (1972) Emanuelson et al. (1973) Johnstone & Rivera (1965)
People in white-collar jobs, whatever their occupational level, tend to participate to a greater extent than manual workers.	Johnstone Z& Rivera (1965) L.O. (1968) SCB (1978)
People who are dissatisfied with their work are more likely to qualify themselves for other occupations than persons who were satisfied with their work. Those who find their work interesting are more likely to participate in education concerning their own professions or trades.	Rubenson (1975)
Regardless of educational background, people who choose stimulating and active leisure activities are mot likely to take part in adult education and non-participants are more likely than participants to go in for passive recreation.	Ingham (1963) Lundahl (1971) Rubenson et al. (1976)
There are likely to be greater discrepancies between expectations and actual socio-economic level or status among full-time adult students than among those not studying, and adult students are more likely to feel relatively deprived, particularly with respect to goals of "fulfilment and satisfaction in work".	Hopper & Osborn (9175)
Adults from the upper social classes follow forms of education which "pay the best" in the form of income, status, occupation, political efficacy.	Hopper & Osborn (1975) Kim (1969)

1. One cannot disgregard the way in which questions about school satisfaction are usually framed. Direct questions such as "How do you lika school?" often lead to the majority answering "Like it very much" (see Kornhauser, 1965).

Althoughy several researchers have taken an interest in the relation between self-perception and achievement, only two previous studies (Denmark and Guttentag, 1967; Stockfelt and Sköld, 1981) directly relate self-perception and participation in adult education, which can be regarded as an expression of achievement. A closer inspection of these works may be worthwhile. The theory that people seek to achieve states agreeing with their views of themselves, of other people, and of their surroundings suggests that those with a positive self-evaluation are more likely to succeed in achievement-oriented situations than those with a negative self-evaluation. Table 6 summarises a number of research findings that support this proposition. In all these studies, some direct attempt has been made to measure self-evaluation, in terms of self-perception, self-respect, self-reliance, self-confidence, or some other cognate concept, such concepts are closely related to one another and can therefore be used together as measures of self-evaluation (silver and Tippett, 1965; Heaton and Duerfeldt, 1973).

It should be mentioned with reference to Table 6, that in a few isolated cases no connection has been found between achievement and self-evaluation (e.g. Dyson, 1967; Trachtman and Denmark, 1973). Generally, however, the self-evaluation concept has been fruitful as a means of explaining achievement-oriented behaviour.

There is no single theory that offers a simple and concrete explanation of why individuals develop different self-evaluations (Sjöstrand, 1974). It is clear, however, that self-evaluation is learned from social interaction. People see themselves by observing the attitudes and valuations they elicit from those around them. Particular importance is attached to the reactions encountered in the people who are important to each person.

One important factor is the extent to which the individual's environment is hierarchically ordered, i.e. the extent to which behaviour is controlled from above (see Korman, 1974). A permissive environment in which the individual is given great scope of action is more likely to lead to the development of a positive self-evaluation. Since our present aim is to try to understand participation in recurrent education, the environments occurring during the life cycle are particularly interesting – the childhood environment, school, and the workplace.

Table 6
STUDIES SUPPORTING THE SUPPOSITION THAT THE HIGHER THE DEGREE OF SELF-RESPECT THE BETTER THE PERFORMANCE IN ACHIEVEMENT-ORIENTED SITUATIONS

Findings	Authors
A comparison of women who had enrolled for adult education and actually started, with women who had completed the enrolment form but not handed it in, revealed that the former had a higher degree of self-confidence than the latter.	Denmark & Guttentag (1967)
Students with a high degree of self-reliance tend more than students with a low degree of self-reliance to choose occupations for which they considered themselves suitable.	Korman (1967a, 1967b)
Women in supervisory positions display a higher self-evaluation than women who are not in such positions.	Morrison & Sebald (1974)
Students with definite vocational plans have a higher degree of self-confidence than those who were uncertain about their plans.	Resnick et al. (1970) Mainer & Herman (1974)
There is a connection between school grades and self-perception.	Brookover & Thomas (1963-64) Coopersmith (1967) Willen (1973) Morrison et al. (1973) Primavera et al. (1974) Sjöstrand (1974)

Previous research has yielded certain evidence that the degree of hierarchy in these environments influences self-evaluation. This is summarised in Table 7. Little attention has been directly focused on how the work environment affects self-evaluation, but the studies in which work performance and social involvement are related to the work situation indirectly give an indication of the connection between the two.

According to Sjöstrand (1974), a person's self-evaluation is relatively stable over time. This need not be taken to imply that the work environment is unimportant on the argument that the childhood and school environments have already "determined" the individual. Rather, there is a relation between the degree of hierarchy in the environment in which one grows up and that which one encounters in working life. It is the direction of self-evaluation that is stable, while the criteria by which one appraises oneself change during the life cycle. As

Table 7
STUDIES SHOWING A CONNECTION BETWEEN CHILDHOOD, SCHOOL, AND WORK ENVIRONMENTS AND SELF–EVALUATION

Findings	Authors
Childhood Environment	
High self-evaluation is connected with low paternal domination during childhood.	McClelland (1961)
The degree of affection in the relationship between father and son is crucial to the identification process.	Rosenberg (1965)
Father identifications is positively related to school results, career aspirations and self-evaluation among high school students.	Jackson et al. (1974)
Teenagers from "democratic" homes have higher educational aspirations than teenagers coming from a hierarchically controlled environment.	Bowerman & Elder (1964)
The self-confidence of young people is positively related to the extemt to which parents had encouraged them to think and act independently.	Coopermith (1967) Rehnberg et al. (1970) Kandel & Lesser (1972)
Young people with low self-evaluation finds greater difficulty in communicaton with their parents than those with a high self-evaluation.	Matteson (1974)
School Environment	
The teacher's self-acceptance or non-acceptance have repercussions on the student's self-evaluation.	Edeburn & Landry (1974)
Students who have taken part in "open classes" have greater self-confidence than those who had followed traditional class instruction.	Sullivan (1974) Franks et al. (1974)
Work Environment	
Work offering little opportunity to influence others is accompanied by a low level of self-confidence.	Kornhauser (1965) Gardell (1971)
Foremen whose work is altered so that they acquire more responsibility and more authority improve their work performance.	Davis & Valper (1968)
There is a positive relation between control of work and production.	Tannenbaum (1962) Bowers (1964)
When persons not normally allowed to participate in decisionmaking and planning are allowed to do so, work performance improves.	Farris (1969)
When the scope for individual initiative at work is limited by factors in the work process, the ability of people to participate in leisure activites posing such demands is also reduced.	Meissner (1971 Sheppard (1972– Bergsten (1977)

Findings	Authors
Interest in participating in the firm's decision-making process rises with self-determination in one's work.	Gardell (1971)
The interest shown by under-educated persons in education relating to their own accupations is governed by their ability to control their own work situation.	Rubenson et al. (1976) Stockfelt & Sköld (1981) Knudsen & Skaalvik (1979)

can be seen from Table 7, changes in the work environment have led to greater activity on the part of the individual. Very simply, an explanation in line with Festinger's and Heider's theories implies that the outward changes in the environment force the individual to change his view of himself and the world around him, and to change his behaviour to prevent dissonance. It should also be pointed out that socialisation does not just stop at some point in each person's life, when he or she becomes a mature member of society (Giddens, 1979).

In summary, therefore, the degree of hierarchy in the current surroundings of the individual, and especially the work situation, appears to play a crucial role in determining expectations about adult education.

The Values of Member Groups and Reference Groups

The value put on adult education is determined by processes, like other valuations, and greatly depends on the past and present environment of the individual. Newcomb's (1950) concepts of member and reference groups are relevant here. The former refers to a group of which the subject is an acknowledged member, e.g. a family or a political or religious group. Individuals share the norms of the group not only because they are acknowledged as members but also because they have learned to satisfy their needs on the basis of the commonly accepted norms. Often, however, people learn norms from other groups of which they are not acknowledged members. This is why Newcomb distinguishes between member groups and reference groups. We may assume that all member groups serve as reference groups, in one way or another, while not all reference groups serve as member groups.

Brunner (1959) touches on the relation between participation in adult education and the norms of the member groups and he refers to a study by Houle (1947) which showed that education programmes based on the interests of individual people reached smaller numbers than those that were based on the pattern of values in the group. Thus it was found that the course preferences of those consulted were determined more by the values of the group than by individual interests. Newcomb's approach is fruitful not only in explaining differences of participation between under-educated and well-educated people, but also when trying to understand differences within the under-educated group. Several studies have shown that white-collar workers, regardless of occupational level, participate in adult education more than manual workers (see table 5). Research by Rubenson (1975) revealed no differences between the two groups with regard to outward impediments, but differences in their attitudes to education did exist.

One possible explanation for the difference in attitudes to education of white-collar and manual workers is that the former are more influenced by people other than their co-workers, who may be regarded as a member group. In many cases it is a matter of people forming a reference group with a positive attitude towards adult education. Moreover, the working group (the member group) has by tradition exerted stronger pressure among manual workers than among those in white-collar jobs. This is discussed by Miller (1967), who observes the conflicts existing in the United States between the values of the working class and those represented by the educational institutions. This conflict is expressed, among other ways, by the indifference of American trade unions to adult education. In Sweden, on the other hand, the trade unions are not merely interested in adult education; they can even be said to lead its development (Broström & Ekeroth, 1977).

We may conclude that people in white-collar occupations find themselves in an educationally more favourable environment because of their greater access to reference groups that hold positive values towards education.

It is clear from both the theoretical approaches and empirical findings discussed above that it is not enough to inform and influence people individually; adult education also has to work through the groups to which the individual belongs and identifies with. This has been made particularly apparent by the experimental outreach work carried out in Sweden. Outreach work when conducted at workplaces, thereby involving the overwhelming majority of the work group, has been far more successful than similar activities conducted in housing areas (SOU, 1974; Broström and Ekerot, 1975 and 1976; Rubenson, 1979). All experiments hitherto underline the importance of outreach work operating through the medium of organisations to which the target people belong, and this implies particular problems for housewives and others based in the home. The circle of friends and the family too are important influences on a person's attitude to adult education (Reese and Paisley, 1968; Molander, 1973; Abrahamsson, 1974).

Discussions that arise from outreach activities at the workplace provide an occasion to talk to colleagues about studying. People who are somewhat hesitant and uncertain may be encouraged by colleagues who are surer about education and have come to realise what education has to offer, which will make it easier for the hesitant to judge whether they have anything to gain by participating.

4. A Proposed Paradigm and Concluding Observations

The Model Itself

In the previous discussion of cognitive models of motivation, it emerged that the probability of an individual's participation in adult education will depend on whether it is seen by that person as a conceivable means of satisfying experienced needs and, further, whether the person believes that he/she can complete the course and successfully cope with it.

Other people will probably not participate. This affords a fruitful point of departure for a model of participation in adult education. It tells us nothing, however, about the "objective world" that influences valence and expectancy. Indeed, there is disagreement about the precise way in which an individual's actual situation influences what Lewin (1951) calls his "current psychological field".

In fact, knowledge about how the individual interprets this psychological field, which is a central aspect of Lewin's theory, cannot by itself give an understanding of recruitment. Only when structural factors and an analysis of the interaction between these and the individual's conceptual apparatus are included does an interpretation of recruitment become possible. In other words, in our model, participation in adult education is regarded as a function of the individual's interpretation of the psychological field as it has developed through interaction with structural factors in society. Through the socialisation that has taken place within the family, school and occupational life, individuals develop certain attitudes towards different forms of adult education. What is then of interest is to identify those factors which may conceivably stimulate or inhibit participation. The degree of hierarchy in the environment and the values of the member and reference groups appear to be of importance (Rubenson, 1976). Other influential factors include the availability of study opportunities, admissions policies, and financial aid systems. Although there are other factors that influence levels of participation, we conclude that hierarchic structure, characteristics of member and reference groups, and actual study possibilities are of general significance and are, therefore, accorded special status in our model. The other main component is the current needs of the individual which, among other things, reflect his/her material situation and the demands made at different stages of the life cycle.

Our model is illustrated in Figure 2 but, like all models, it is simplified. The three groups of intervening independent variables – active preparedness, structural factors, and current needs – are not mutually independent. Recruitment cannot always be explained directly on the basis of the individual's situation without taking into account how he or she interprets that situation. In the model, this is shown by the two levels of intermediate variables. The first level comprises active preparedness, perception, and interpretation of the structural factors and experienced needs. These variables in turn determine the second level comprising valence and expectancy, which together result in a force. The strength of this force, in relation to other forces acting on the individual, determines whether or not the individual will actually participate in adult education.

Figure 2
PARADIGM OF RECRUITMENT IN ADULT EDUCATION

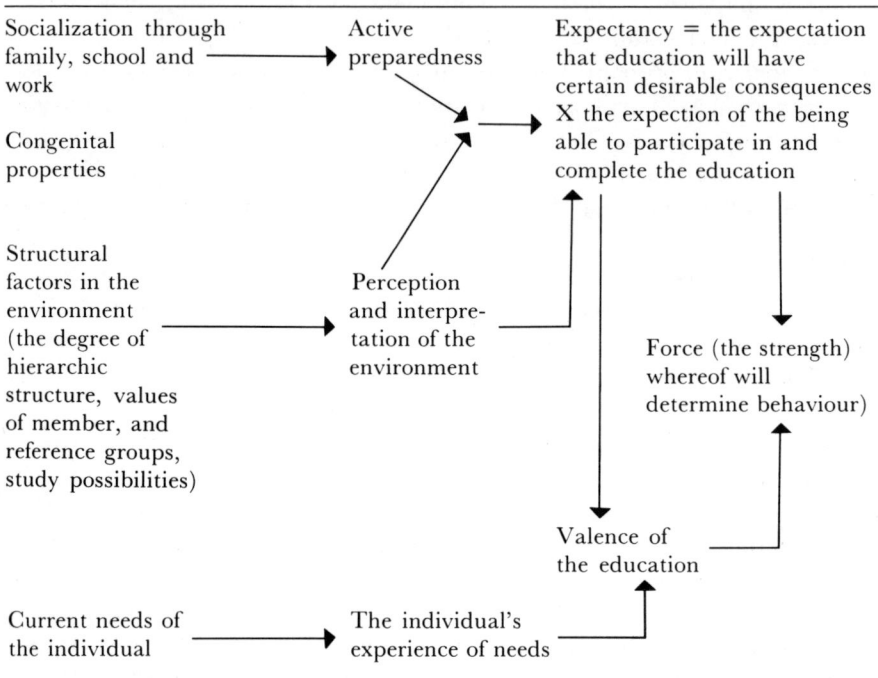

Mathematically, the relationship between valence, expectancy, and force can be expressed as follows:

$$K = f \left[\sum_{i=1}^{n} (V_i \times F_i) \right]$$

K = force conducive to an action;
V_i = valence for the conceivable consequences of the action;
F_i = expectation that the action will have those consequences.

The purpose of our model is not to produce a mathematical description of recruitment in adult education but to give a general indication of how to relate structural to individual factors. In this way, the model can suggest directions for future research and serve as a basis for the interpretation and collation of previous research. Its value will depend on how well it can serve these purposes and here we will apply it to research on why adult education has up to now increased the educational gap rather than the reverse.

The Model Applied to Existing Research Results

– Active Preparedness

An outstanding problem in this field is how to account for the fact that initial educational level consistently shows the highest correlation with participation in adult education. To some extent, of course, it depends on the fact that the highly-educated are often in occupational positions that offer opportunities for participation in different forms of education (for example, SCB, 1978). Available studies show, however, that the differences are very large even for non-vocational adult education (SCB, 1978; Bunnage and Hedegaard; Knudsen and Skaalvik, 1979; Cross, 1979).

This can be explained by the socialisation that has taken place within the family, the school and, later on, in working life. Within this configuration of instances, adult education becomes a part of the value system of certain groups but not of others. Participation in non-vocational adult education, for example, is one aspect of a leisure style consisting of cultural activities that is typically found in the middle and upper classes (Bergsten, 1977; Knudsen and Skaalvik, 1979).

The school is often blamed for this social bias in participation, but simply to accord blame is not very fruitful. It is more constructive to use the insights of educational sociology to clarify what functions the school has in society and to analyse how the curriculum and teaching process transfer value systems to the individual (see Lundgren, 1979). It can be added that analyses of the education system and its functions in society have not given much attention to the adult education sector (see Karabel and Halsey, 1977) even though it is impossible, at least in Scandinavia, to analyse the role of education in determining the division of power in society without considering the part played by popular education. In any event, it can be concluded that active preparedness, by itself, does not determine participation in adult education but acts in combination with structural factors.

– Structural Factors

Structural factors tend to strengthen already established inequalities. So, in line with our model, those with a high degree of active preparedness tend to be in environments which give them scope for influencing their situation (i.e. a low degree of hierarchic structure). Their member and reference groups tend to be positive towards adult education, and moreover they have – relatively – the best access to education.

If, for the sake of analysis, we regard the differences in active preparedness as constant (of course it can change as the surrounding world does), then the focus is turned to what changes can be achieved through structural factors and what significance these ultimately have in counteracting the accumulated inequalities that have been established over time. Let us look at two areas: a) working life, b) study possibilities.

a) *Working Life*

The literature on the psychology of work points to a link between technological changes and an individual's attitude to activities such as education. In the Swedish Commission on Low Incomes both quantitative and qualitative differences in life-pattern were established between those with good and bad working conditions – good and bad with respect to "sweat, dirt and physical exhaustion" (Lundahl, 1971). Meissner (1971) succeeded in demonstrating a direct correlation between job design and the individual's life outside work. When the scope for personal initiative on the job is limited by factors in the work process, an individual's ability to participate during leisure time in activities which make such demands decrease. A corresponding tendency emerges concerning the effect of work with limited opportunities for social contact. Meissner concluded that "when questions are put which are designed to find out what people actually do with their time and if they have control over the space, time, and function of their work, the job has a long arm indeed".

When employees are given increased influence over their own work they show greater interest in participating in decision-making processes. Such changes also influence their leisure-time activities and lead to more active leisure (Gardell, 1976, Bergsten, 1977). There is, accordingly, a strong correlation between an individual's possibility of controlling his/her situation and participation in adult education (Knudsen and Skaalvik, 1979).

Two parallel lines of development can be observed in adult education referring to changes in working life. If we disregard the education given in companies' industrial schools, it is today mainly white-collar groups who have the possibility of gaining a relatively broad education as part of their job. However, if far-reaching reforms in working life come about, a broad general education for more groups will be required (see Skard, 1977). This may well take place through direct association with work places. Another development that should be expected is a stronger link between gainful employment and the education society offers; for instance, the right to paid leave for studies and increased elements of general education within the framework of personnel training gained through negotiation.

In order to assess the feasibility of realising the redistributive goals of adult education and industrial democracy, we should not yield to rhetoric but instead follow developments closely. The studies of living conditions that the Swedish Bureau of Statistics has undertaken since the autumn of 1974 – the ULF statistics – shed light on these questions.

Of particular interest is the line taken by the trade unions. Thoroughgoing changes in the educational situation of workers will probably require, among other things, greater involvement of trade union organisations in matters of recurrent education. One step in this direction is for the trade unions to endeavour, by means of legislation or collective bargaining, to gain added control of education. They should be capable of playing an important part in bringing about a scheme of adult education that is conducive to systematic change and which improves collective conditions. As was stated by the Swedish Confederation of Trade Unions (LO Working Committee on Adult Education, Report No. 4, 1976), the large majority of adults in ordinary occupations and social conditions cannot improve their situation by means of personal careers – by "doing something else". Nor should they rest content with improvements within the framework of existing conditions. Instead, the trade unions advocate the transformation of society by collective efforts.

b) *Study Possibilities*

The theory underlying our model suggests that participation is very much dependent on whether the individual sees any value in education. One of the explanations of why education has had disappointing equalising effects is that advantaged groups have too much influence on patterns of provision. This is exacerbated by the lack of precise statements of redistributive policy goals (Broström and Ekeroth, 1977). An analysis of recruitment to workers' voluntary educational associations shows that even an organisation with pronounced redistributive policy ambitions actually makes provision that corresponds best to the demands of the advantaged (Finstad and Hansen, 1976). One contributing factor is that the existing pattern of subsidies does not compensate for the increased costs involved in recruiting the underprivileged.

Recruitment problems should not be seen only as reflecting failures in information about existing provision. This was demonstrated by a survey of study needs and obstacles among the under-educated (Rubenson et al., 1976). In spite of the availability of a wide selection of courses, a large group stated that they had no opportunities of studying the course they desired. Closer examination of the actual provision showed that although these views partly reflected ignorance of opportunities, it was also a reflection of deficiencies in the range of available opportunities. The most revealing finding, given that the study was concerned with workers with low levels of education, was the great interest they took in education relating to their present occupations. The data suggest that this type of interest is not mainly a bid for advancement but evidence of a desire to master more thoroughly the tasks involved in the present job, even though the workers cope with them satisfactorily already. This may be due to a desire for greater job satisfaction or else to an apprehension of failure.

This study suggested, therefore, that existing programmes should be supplemented by study circles connected to the work role, which can help participants to view their work situation in a broader context as well as supplying them with vocational knowledge. The study associations would have to show an interest not only in liberal and trade union education but also in occupationally-related educational programmes.

Future Research

Research hitherto can be divided into two categories: (i) studies describing participants in certain types of adult education; (ii) studies comparing characteristics of participants and non-participants. Both types of research have shown that recruitment in adult education is biased and that special measures will have to be taken in order to reach the under-educated. On the other hand, the studies have yielded only superficial knowledge of the factors that influence participation and this has limited the possibilities of taking adequate measures in this field. The observation that higher social classes participate more than lower ones is valuable in itself, but it makes only a limited contribution towards the explanation of recruitment problems.

Since the purpose of most research in this field has been to study the effects of previous education, social and regional factors, age, and sex, almost the entire focus of attention has been on differences between various sub-groups of the population. The existence of substantial variations within these groups has tended to be overlooked. Yet, there are cases where under-educated people participate and the well-educated do not. This suggests, according to Douglas and Moss (1968), that future analysis of educational participation by adults should "investigate the differential participation patterns exhibited within what are generally assumed to be relatively homogenous groups."

In this connection, a more dynamic approach needs to be adopted in the realisation that variables such as age, education level, and so on, are per se of subordinate importance. The paradigm in Figure 2 suggests that it would be more profitable to investigate the preparedness of people for participation, the environment in which they live, the forces in these environments that stimulate or inhibit participation, and their dominant needs. In other words, participation should be viewed in terms of the total living situation of individuals.

The model assumes that recurrent education is one of several means whereby people, individually or collectively, are able to satisfy some of their needs and meet the demands made on them. Needs and demands change as the individual moves through life. Thus, one explanation for the relatively low participation of the under-educated may be that the education offered is not relevant to them. It may also be that the education offered could fulfil this function but that the potential target group fails to realise this and entertains a low expectation of what it can lead to. Accordingly, one possible line of further research would be to chart the needs and demands individuals experience and to ascertain if they see education as a means of satisfying those needs, and what this kind of education should be. Instead of a conventional investigation of interest in existing education routes (which many people have no idea about in any case) the task will be to plot the roles of the individuals – in the family, during leisure hours, as a member of society and in the labour market – and to study educational needs and expectancy in terms of these roles. This strategy can be seen as one step towards a third phase of research on participation (the first phase being the description of those who take part, and the second the comparison of participants and non-participants).

Another topic for research is the expectancy concept. One way of investigating this is illustrated in Figure 3 which is based on the more general model outlined in Figure 2. This structure can also serve as a starting point for the charting of impediments to recruitment.

The suggestions for further research mentioned so far are for studies of an exploratory character. There is, however, another type of research that intervenes in and influences the experience of the individual and in doing so observes the effect on expectancy, valence, and participation. This presupposes the close association of researchers and those responsible for the conduct of education. As Glaser (1973) observes, "the behavioural and social sciences are at a point in their development where they absolutely require the direction and disciplining effects that come from contact with real-world problems".

Figure 3
DESIGN FOR INVESTIGATING THE EXPECTANCY CONCEPT

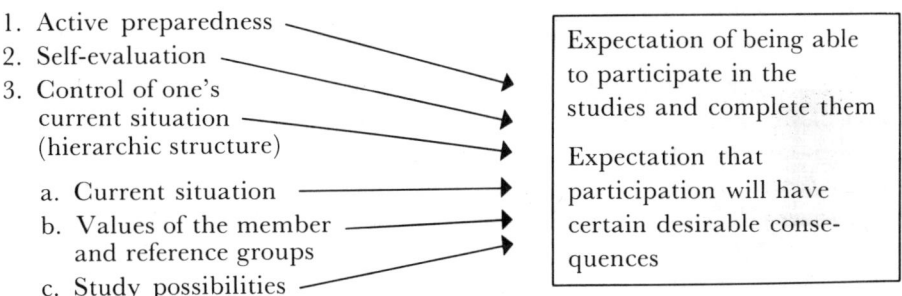

One possible example of this would be a combination of the practical experiments conducted by the Swedish Committee on Methods Testing in Adult Education in the form of outreach work, and exploratory studies of the kind referred to above. Educational needs and recruitment impediments would first be plotted. This should be done before the outreach work begins. Phase two would involve outreach work, the education offered being geared as closely as possible in terms of content, design, and conduct to the demands that emerge from the exploratory phase. An investigation of this kind would make it possible to arrive at a deeper understanding of the way in which the different factors in our model are related to each other and to participation in adult education, and it would provide the evidence on which to base changes.

Another example would be to alter the individual's environment so as to give him/her greater control over his/her situation. This is especially relevant with regard to the working environment (as the next chapter discusses in detail). In terms of our model, the question arises of how the nature of given forms of industrial democracy and the ability of the trade unions to influence and supervise education, opportunities for educational leave, etc., influence the factors of expectancy and valence. One line of study would be to investigate the extent to which increased influence via industrial democracy affects attitudes towards trade union education. Assuming other factors to be constant, one might expect greater influence at the workplace to increase the likelihood of participation in trade union education having positive consequences.

Practical Implications of the Model

As Kurt Lewin so rightly remarked, "there is nothing so practical as a good theory". Unfortunately, we do not have a good theory, but only a basic model. Nonetheless, this can be useful, even to practitioners, since it underlines the importance of gearing education to the living situation of the target group, and of responding to needs and demands, thereby influencing the situation of the individual. There is a general need within the organisations that run education for a partial reassessment of the means that are used for the attainment of their goals. New ways must be tried to supplement existing opportunities for adult education. In doing so, an effort must be made to get away from the traditional subject divisions, and instead be guided by the composite situation of needs and problems which the intended participant experiences. As stated above, the creation of this type of education will demand close co-operation between researchers and providers.

Our model can also provide a basis upon which to explain the experience derived from practical experiments, such as those concerned with outreach work, and also for attempts to generalise such experience. One topic that might be studied is the variability of the results of outreach work, depending on whether they have been conducted in housing areas or at work places. One reason for the superior success of the latter variety may be that it involves a whole member reference group – the work group. The general concepts underlying our model, we believe, should be and are capable of forming the basis for a variety of practical measures and reforms in the field of adult education.

BIBLIOGRAPHY

ABRAHAMSSON, K, (1974), *Kom igen Svensson,* (Let's Do It Svensson) Studentlitteratur, Lund.

ABRAHAMSSON, K., and RUBENSON, K., (1981), "Higher Education and the Lost Generation – Some Comments on Adult Students, Knowledge Ideals and Educational Design in Swedish Post-Secondary Education". Meeting of the Programme on Institutional Management in Higher Education, 18-20 May 1981, CERI/OECD, Paris.

ATKINSON, J., and RAYNOR, J., (Ed.), (1974), *Motivation and Achievement*, V.H. Winstons & Sons, Washington D.C.

BERGSTEN, U., (1977), *Adult Education in Relation to Work and Leisure*, Almqvist & Wiksell International, Stockholm.

BOSHIER, R., (1971), "Motivational Orientations of Adult Education Participants: A Factor Analytic Exploration of Houle's Typology", *Adult Education*, 21, 3-26.

BOSHIER, R., (1973), "Educational Participation and Dropout: A Theoretical Model", *Adult Education*, 23, 255-282.

BOWERMAN, C., and ELDER, G., (1964), "Variations in Adolescent Perception of Family Power Structure", *American Sociological Review*, 29, 551-567.

BOWERS, D., (1964), "Organisational Control in an Insurance Company", *Sociometry*, 27, 230-244.

BROOKOV ER, W., and THOMAS, S., (1963-64), "Self-Concept of Ability and School Achievement", *Sociology of Education*, 37, 27-28.

BROSTRÖM, A. and EKEROTH, G., (1975), "Utvärdering av försök med uppsökande verksamhet inon kommunal vuxenutbildning", (Evaluation of an Outreach Experiment in Municipal Adult Education) Vt-74, Department of Sociology, Uppsala.

BROSTRÖM, A., and EKEROTH, G., (1976), "Uppsökande verksamhet inom vuxenutbildningen ur fördelningspolitiskt perspektive", (Outreach Activities in Adult Education in View of Allocation Policy), Department of Sociology, Uppsala.

BROSTRÖM, A., and EKEROTH, G., (1977), "Vuxenutbildning och fördelningspolitik", (Adult Education and Allocation Policy), Department of Sociology, Uppsala.

BRUNNER, E.S. (1959), *An Overview of Adult Education Research*, Adult Education Association, Chicago.

BUHLER, C., (1959), "Theoretical Observations about Life's Basic Tendencies", *American Journal of Psychotherapy*, 13, 561-581.

BUNNAGE, D., and HEDEGAARD, B., (1978), "Voksenuddannelse" (Adult Education), Socialforskningsinstituttet: 81, Köpenhavn.

COFER, C., and APPLEY, M., (1964), *The Antecedents of Self-Esteem*, W.H. Freeman and Company, San Francisco.

COOPERS MITH, S., (1967), *The Antecedents of Self-Esteem*, W.H. Freeman and Company, San Francisco.

CROSS, K.P., (1979), "Adult Learners Characteristics, Needs and Interests", in Petersen, R.E. (Ed.), *Lifelong Learning in America*, Jossey-Bass Publishers, San Francisco.

CROSS, K.P., (1981), *Adults as Learners*, Jossey-Bass Publishers, San Francisco.

DAVIS, L., and VALPER, E., (1968), "Studies in Supervisory Job Designs", *Human Relations*, 19, 339-347.

DENMARK, F., and GUTTENTAG, M., (1967), "Dissonance in the Self-Concepts and Educational Concepts of College and Non-College Oriented Women", *Journal of Counselling Psychology*, 14, 113-115.

DEUTSCH, M., (1954), "Field Theory in Social Psychology", in Lindzey (Ed.), *Handbook of Social Psychology*, Vol. 1, Addison-Wesley Publishing Company, Inc., London.

DOUGLAS, M., and MOSS, G., (1968), "Differential Participation of Adults of Low and High Educational Attainment", *Adult Education*, 18, 247-259.

DYSON, E., (1967), "A Study of Ability-Grouping and the Self-Concept", *The Journal of Educational Research*, 60, 403-405.

DUMEZEDIER, J., (1974), *Sociology of Leisure*, Elsevier, New York.

EDEBURN, C., and LANDRY, R., (1974), "Self-Concepts of Students and a Significant Other, the Teacher", *Psychological Reports*, Vol. 35 (1, Pt. 2), 505-506.

EMANUELSSON, I., FAGERLIND, I., and HARTMAN, S., (1973), "Vuxenutbildning och arbetsförhållanden" (Adult Education and Working Conditions), Report No. 96 on *Education and Psychology*, Institute of Education, Stockholm.

FARRIS, G., (1969), "Organisational Factors and Individual Performance: A Longitudinal Study", *Journal of Applied Psychology*, 53, 87-91.

FESTING ER, L. (1957), *A Theory of Cognitive Dissonance*, Row Peterson and Company, Evanston, Illinois.

FINSTAD, N., and HANSEN, H., (1976), *Voksenoppläring for hvem?* (Adult Education for Whom?), Tidens förlag AOF, Oslo.

FRANKS, D., MARROTTA, J., and DILLON, S., (1974), "Intrinsic Motivation and Feelings of Competency Among Students", *Journal of Research & Development in Education*, 8, 20-29.

GAGE, N., (1963), "Paradigms for Research on Teaching", in Gage, N. (Ed.), *Handbook of Research on Teaching*, Rand McNally & Company, Chicago.

GARDELL, B., (1971), *Produktionsteknik och arbetsglädje* (Means of Production and Work Satisfaction), PA-rådet, Stockholm.

GARDELL, B., (1976), "Psykosociala problem sammanhängande med industriella produktionsprocesser" (Psycho-social Problems Related to Industrial Production Processes), in SOU Reports, Oslo. Reports: Psycho-social Factors.

GIDDENS, A., (1979), *Central Problems in Social Theory*, MacMillan, London.

GLASER, R., (1973), "Educational Psychology and Education", *American Psychologist*, 28, 557-558.
HAVIGHURST, R., (1970), "Changing Status and Roles during the Adult Life Cycle", in Burns, M. (Ed.), *Sociological Backgrounds of Adult Education*, Chicago, CSLEA.
HEATON, R., and DUERFELDT, P., (1973), "The Relationship between Self-Esteem, Self-Reinforcement and the Internal-External Personality Dimension", *Journal of Genetic Psychology*, 123, 3-13.
HEIDER, F., (1958), *The Psychology of Interpersonal Relations*, John Wiley & Sons, Inc., New York.
HIEMSTR A, P.R., (1972), "Continuing Education for the Aged: A Survey of Needs and Interests of Older People", *Adult Education*, 22, 100-109.
HOPPER, E., and OSBORN, M., (1975), *Adult Students*, Frances Pinder, London.
HOULE, C., (1961), *The Inquiring Mind*, The University of Wisconsin Press, Madison.
HUSEN, T., (1969), *Talent, Opportunity and Career*, Almqvist & Wiksell, Uppsala.
INGHAM, R.J., (1963), "The Measurement of Educative Behaviour and its Relationship to the Leisure Satisfactions of College Alumni", Chicago, Ph.D. Thesis, University of Chicago.
JACKSON, R., MEARA, N., and AONA, M., (1974), "Faster Identification, Achievement, and Occupational Behaviour of Rural Youth", *Journal of Vocational Behaviour*, 4, 85-96.
JOHANSSON, L., and EKERWALD, H., (1976), *Vuxenstudier och livssituation* (Adult Education and Life Situation), Prisma, Stockholm.
JOHANSSON, R., (1973), "Studiecirkel 1970. Klientelundersökning avseende studiecirklarna inom de 12 studieförbunden (Study Circle 1970, Study of Clientele in 12 Study Associations), Department of Education, Uppsala.
JOHNSTONE, J., and RIVERA, R., (1965), *Volunteers for Learning*, Study of the Educational Pursuits of American Adults, Aldine, Chicago.
KAMIENSKI, A., (1975), *Vuxenstuderande vid universitet* (Adult Students of the University), Office of Education, Lund.
KANDEL, D., and LESSER, G., (1972), *Youth in Two Worlds*, Jossey-Bass, Inc., London.
KARABEL, J., and HALSEY, A.H., (Ed.), (1977), *Power and Ideology in Education*, Oxford University Press, New York.
KARL, C ., (1979), "Motivationsforschung: Probleme und Ergebnisse der Erforschung von Weiterbildungsmotivation", in Sierbert, H. (Ed.), *Taschenbuch der Weiterbildungsforschung*, Burgbücherei Wilhelm Schneider, Baltmannsweiler.
KIM, L., (1979), *Två års erfarenheter av de nya tillträdesreglerna till högskoleutbildning* (Two Years' Experience with the New Rules of Access to Higher Education),

National Board of Colleges and Universities, 1979, 13, Stockholm.
KNOX, A ., (1970), "Factors related to Educative Activity by Non-College-Bound Young Adults", Teachers College, Columbia University, New York.
KNUDSEN, K., and SKAALVIK, E., (1979), "Deltagelse i voksenopplaering. Noen central fordelninger" (Participation in Adult Education, Some Major Trends), Norwegian Institute of Adult Education Trondheim.
KOCH, S ., (1959), (Ed.), *Psychology: A Study of a Science,* Vol. 2, McGraw-Hill, New York.
KORMAN, A., (1967a), "Self-Esteem as a Moderator of the Relationship between Self-Perceived Abilities and Vocational Choice", *Journal of Applied Psychology,* 51, 65-67.
KORMAN, A., (1967b), "Ethical Judgements, Self-Perceptions and Vocational Choice", in *Proceedings, 75th Annual Convention,* APA, Washington D.C.
KORMAN, A., (1974), *The Psychology of Motivation,* Prentice-Hall, Englewood Cliffs, New Jersey.
KORNHAU SER, A., (1965), *Mental Health of the Industrial Worker,* John Wiley & Sons, Inc., New York.
LECKY, P., (1945), *Self-Consistency: A Theory of Personality,* Island Press, New York.
LEHTONEN, H., and TUOMISTO, J., (1974), "On the Theoretical Background of the Adult Education Survey in Finland, 1972-73, *Adult Education in Finland,* 11:1, 13-19.
LEVIN, H.A., and SCHÜTZE, H.G., (Eds.), 1983, *Financing Recurrent Education: Strategies for Increasing Employment, Job Opportunities and Productivity,* Sage, Beverly Hills.
LEWIN, K., (Cartwright, D., Ed.), (1951), "Field Theory in Social Science", *Selected Theoretical Papers,* Harper & Brothers, New York.
L.O. SWEDISH CONFEDERATION OF LABOUR (1968), "LO-Medlemmen Och Utbildningsfrågorna", (The LO-Member and Education, Report of the Swedish Confederation of Labour's Committee on Adult Education), Stockholm.
LONDON, J., (1970), "The Influence of Social Class Behaviour upon Adult Education Participation", *Adult Education,* 20, 140-153.
LONDON, J., WENCKERT, R., and HAGSTRÖM, W., (1963), "Education and Social Class", Survey Research Center, University of California, Berkeley.
LUNDAHL, A., (1971), *Fritid och rekreation,* (Leisure Time and Recreation), Allmänna Förlaget, Stockholm.
LUNDGREN, U., (1979), "Background; The Conceptual Framework", in Lundgren, U., and Patterson, S., Ed.), *Code Context and Curriculum Processes,* Studies in Education and Psychology, SIE, Stockholm.

LYNN, D., (1962), "Sex Role and Parental Identification", *Child Development*, 33, 555-564.
MADSEN, K., (1968), "Theories of Motivation", Kent State University, Kent.
MANSFIELD, R., (1973), "Self-Esteem, Self-Perceived Abilities and Vocational Choice", *Journal of Vocational Behaviour*, 3, 433-441.
MAIER, D., and HERMAN, A., (1974), "The Relationship of Vocational Decidedness and Satisfaction with Dogmatism and Self-Esteem", *Journal of Vocational Behaviour*, 5, 95-102.
MATTERSON, R., (1974), "Adolescent Self-Esteem, Family Communication, and Marital Satisfaction", *Journal of Psychology*, 86, 35-47.
McCLELLAND, D., (1961), *The Achieving Society*, Van Nostrand, Princeton, New Jersey.
MEISSNER, M., (1971), "The Long Arm of the Job: A Study of Work and Leisure", *Industrial Relations*, 10, 239-260.
MEZIROW, J., (1971), "Toward a Theory of Practice in Education with Particular Reference to the Education of Adults", *Adult Education*, 21, 135-147.
MILLER, H., (1967), "Participation af Adults in Education", Mass. Center for the Study of Liberal Education for Adlts, Brookline.
MOLANDER, L.G., (1973). "Vuxna 1970, Erfarenheter och Intresse av Vuxundervisning", (Adults 1970, Participation and Interest in Adult Education), Department of Education, Uppsala.
MORRISON. I., RHOMAS, D., and WEAVER, S., (1973), "Self-Esteem and Self-Estimates of Academic Performance", *Journal of Consulting & Clinical Psychology, 41, 412-415.*
MORRISON, R., and SEBALD, M.L., *(1974)*, *"Personal Characteristics Differentiating Female Executive from Female Non-Executive Personnel", Journal of Applied Psychology, 59, 656-659.*
NEWCOMB, T., *(1950)*, *Social Psychology*, The Dryden Press, New York.
NIAE (917), "Adequacy of Provision", *Adult Education*, 42:6, London.
OECD (1975a), *Education, Inequality and Life Chances*, Paris.
OECD/CERI (1975b), *Recurrent Education: Trends and Issusssses*, Paris.
OECD/CERI (1976), *Developments in Educational Leave of Absence*, Paris.
OECD/CERI (1978), *Alternation between Work and Education – A Study of Educational Leave of Absence at Enterprise Level*, Paris.
OLOFSSON, L.E., (1981), "The Relationship between Schooling and Adult Education in the Context of Lifelong Learning", paper presented at International Colloquium on Policy and Research in Adult Education, (5–11 July 1981), University of Nottingham.
PARKER, E., and PAISLEY, W., (1966), "Patterns of Adult Information Seeking", Stanford University, Stanford, California.
PRIMAVERA, L., SIMON, W., and PRIMAVERA, A., (1974), "The Re-

lationship between Self-Esteem and Academic Achievement: An Investigation of Sex Differences", *Psychology in the Schools*, 11, 213-216.

REES, M., and PAISLEY, W., (1968), "Social and Psychological Predictors of Adult Information and Media Use, *Adult Education*, 19, 11-29.

REHBERG, E., SINCLAIR, J., amd SCHAEFER, W., (1970). "Adolescent Achievement Behaviour, Family Authority Structure, and Parental Socialisation Practices", *American Journal of Sociology*, 75, 1012-1034.

RESNICK, H., FAUBLE, M., and OSIPOW, S., (1970), "Vocational Crystallisation and Self-Esteem in collage Students", *Journal of Counselling Psychology*, 17, 465-467.

ROBINSON, R., (1970), "Participation in and Industrial Area of West Milwaukee", *Adult Education*, 20, 226-232.

ROGERS, C., (1959), "A Theory of Therapy, Personality and Interpersonal Relationships, as Developed in the Client-Centered Framework". In Koch, S., (Ed.), *Psychology: The Study of a Science*, Vol. 3, McGraw-Hill, New York.

ROSENBERG, M., (1965), "Society and the Adolescent Self-Image", Princeton University Press, Princeton.

RUBENSON, K., (1972), "Intresse för Vuxentbildning Bland Unga Män med Kortutbildning" (Interest in Adult Education Among Young, Less Educated Males), Department of Education, Göteborg.

RUBENSON, K., (1975), Rekrytering till Vuxenutbildning. En Studie Av Kortutbildade Yngre Män (Recruitment for Adult Education – A Study of Young, Less Educated Adults), Acta Universitatis, Göteborg.

RUBENSON, K., (1986), "Recruitment in Adult Education: A Research Strategy", Department of Educational Research, 3/1976, Stockholm.

RUBENSON, K., (1979), "Recruitment to Adult Education in the Nordic Countries – Research and Outreaching Activities", Reports on Education and Psychology 3/1979, Stockholm Institute of Education, Stockholm.

RUBENSON, K., BERGSTEN, L., and BROMSJO, B., (1976), "The Attitude of the Under-Educated Towards Adult Education", Institute of Education 6/1975, Stockholm.

SHEPPARD, H., (1972), *Where Have All The Robots Gone?* Free Press, New York.

SILLBER, E., and Tippett, J., (1965), "Self-Esteem: clinical Assessment and Measurement Validation", *Psychological Reports*, 16, 1017-1071.

SJÖSTRAND, C., (1974), "Grundskolemiljö och Tonårselevers Självvärdering" (The Comprehensive School Environment and the Students' Self-Concept of themselves), Department of Education, Göteborg

SCB/SWEDISH CENTRAL BUREAU OF STATISTICS (1978), "Living Conditions", Report 14, Adult Education, Employment, SCB, Stockholm.

SOU/SWEDISH GOVERNMENT OFFICIAL REPORTS, (1974) N° 54, "Vidgad Vuxenutbildning" (Extended Adult Education).

SOU/SWEDISH GOVERNMENT OFFICIAL REPORTS, (1977) N° 92,

"Utbildning i Företag, Kommuner och Landsting" (Education within Enterprises, Municipalities and Regions).

STOCKFELT, T., and SKÖLD, M., (1981), "Everyday Learning – The Basis for Adult Education", Brevskolan, Stockholm.

SULLIVAN, J., (1974), "Open – Traditional – What is the Difference", *Elementary School Journal*, 74, 493-500.

TANNEENBAUM, A., (1962), "Control in Organisations, Individual Adjustment and Organisational Performance", *Administrative Science Quarterly*, 7, 236-257.

TAUGH, A., (1969), "Some Major Reasons for Learning", in *Self-Concept in Adult Participation*, Conference Report, ERIC, Ed. 033252.

TRACHTMAN, J., and DENMARK, F., (1973), "Self-Esteem and Other Motivational Variables: Some Black-White Comparisons", *International Journal of Group Tensions*, 3, 136-143.

TURNSTALL, J., (1974), *The Open University Opens*. Routledge and Kegan Paul, London.

WILLEN, B., (1973), "Attityder, Värderingar Och Fritidssysselsättningar Hos 14- och 16-åringar i Göteborg, Samt En Skolsystemjämförelse'" (Attitudes, Values and Leisure-Time Activities Among 14–16-Year-Olds and a Comparison of School Systems in Göteborg), Department of Education, Göteborg.

VROOM, V., (1964), *Work and Motivation*, John Wiley, New York.

Chapter IV
RECURRENT EDUCATION AND INDUSTRIAL DEMOCRACY*

1. Background to an Analysis

It is against a background of profound flux and uncertainty that the current interest in industrial democracy must be placed and ultimately its implications for education, particularly for recurrent education (1).

A brief historical glance may help to impose some pattern on developments relevant to democracy up to the present day. The first step was the emergence of formal political democracy through the progressive attainment of universal suffrage and the evolution of democratic institutions. Second came the legitimation of the right to a certain standard of living and a concern for greater equality, which may be termed welfare democracy. It is at least plausible to suggest that we have now entered a third stage, where the question of democratic control over economic decisions occupies a central position. Whether this is labelled economic democracy or industrial democracy is largely a matter of choice, but it is the latter term which is generally accepted as having the larger compass.

We make no attempt in what follows to stipulate a tight definition of industrial democracy. What we are basically concerned with here is the distribution and shifts of power within the workplace and the economy, as between labour, management and the owners of capital, and the implications for the immediate focus of this book – recurrent education.

For the distribution of power is shifting. The right of capital owners and their representatives to take all the decisions that determine the volume, distribution, and nature of work and its consequences for society is no longer accepted as absolute. Major changes have taken place through legislation or through the collective bargaining process. However, this shift in the distribution of power is by no means a steady and assured process and contemporary interest is no guarantee of lasting achievement.

The first major upsurge of interest in industrial democracy came with the First World War and the period of reconstruction which followed it, but chang-

---

* Grateful acknowledgement is made of the assistance rendered by the Group of Specialists convened to advise the Centre on this aspect of the recurrent education project. Its members were Dr. Eric Batstone, Department of Social and Administrative Studies, University of Oxford; Dr. Pierre Caspar, former Directeur de l'Education Quaternaire, France, and currently Professor at the Conservatoire National des Arts et Mâtiers, Paris; Dr. Nadio Delai, Director of CENSIS, Rome, Italy; Professor Hans Pornschlegel, Sozialakademie, Dortmund, West Germany; Dr. Oyvind Skard, former Director of Training, Norwegian Employers Confederation, Oslo; and Mr. Roland Svensson, Director, Arbetslivcentrum, Stockholm. Each member of the Group contributed a paper, and it is on these (which were individual contributions and not official reports) that this chapter is based.

ing economic conditions, the onset of the Great Depression, and the buildup to another war stunted further development. With the end of the Second World War came a resurgence of interest and action. In Norway, the unity created by the war and the underground movement gave fresh impetus to co-operation between management and labour; legislation on works councils and co-determination was passed in Germany; and in the United Kingdom, nationalisation and the growth of consultative organisations gave support to the idea of a new distribution of decision-making powers within industry.

Again, however, the impetus was not sustained, although in some countries more than others there was a continuation of the power-sharing process. Economic growth and prosperity meant that the emphasis was placed more on distributional aspects, under the approach we have referred to as welfare democracy. Citizens' rights and expectations were construed primarily in terms of consumption, and both governmental policy and trade union efforts were focused on achieving broader access to material wealth. During the fifties and sixties, therefore, relatively little was heard of industrial democracy.

It is worth pointing briefly to some of the factors which — to different degrees in different countries — are now pushing governments, trade unions and (largely as a reaction) employers into considering and developing their policies in this area. First, there is a growing concern for the qualitative aspects of working life. This concern emerged before the current crisis as an awareness that people do not work only to provide for their material wants but the nature of their work is central to the intrinsic satisfaction they derive from life. Under conditions of full employment, most of the emphasis was placed at the level of the work group, and on improving the working environment of the individual employee, not least as regards occupational health and the physical dangers of new chemicals.

Second, there was a shift of focus away from the citizen as consumer and over to the citizen as producer. During the past two decades, material rewards and increased leisure time were regarded as compensating the individual worker for poor working conditions and few opportunities for responsibility at the place of work. This approach is now seen to be grossly deficient, and ignores the way in which the individual's working conditions influence the whole of his or her life — the "long arm of the job", as it has been termed. Many of the continuing social and cultural inequalities are inextricably interwoven with inequalities within the production process. Recognition of this fact is particularly relevant to any consideration of the potential of recurrent education.

Third, attitudes towards technology have changed. The idea that technological developments have their own internal logic which cannot be challenged or diverted has lost ground, and the inevitability of given technological changes has been questioned. Deriving directly from this is the question of whether humans adjust to meet the demands of technology or whether technology is developed to meet human needs. Power over decisions on the character and impact of technological development is, therefore, now very much at the forefront of debate. The critical implication is that choices are involved, and that these choices should be open to democratic decision-making.

The notion that technological changes are themselves subject to control and conscious decision, instead of being autonomous and inevitable, finds a parallel in the trade unions' growing appreciation of the scope of collective bargaining. In the face of large-scale redundancies and rationalisations, the labour movement is increasingly aware that the decisions that lead up to such events are often taken months or even years previously, and so far have fallen outside the negotiating arena. They are, therefore, engaged in extending the scope of collective bargaining, bringing into it areas of company policy that have hitherto been regarded as the sole prerogative of management.

Perhaps the most prominent example is that of so-called "rationalisation": decisions to invest in labour-saving equipment have inevitable consequences for large parts of the work force, and once those investments have been made, future employment patterns are very largely determined, even if there often remains considerable latitude for bargaining over terms and conditions. The more prescient unions have taken their reasoning one step further, and are seeking to influence the nature of the research processes which lead up to investment decisions, at least in the sense of pressing for the inclusion of criteria other than purely financial ones. The development of "alternative corporate plans" and the notion of socially useful production are also to be seen in this context.

Conversely, management too sees reasons for encouraging some forms of participation. Given high levels of capital intensity, the interruption of production becomes an increasingly costly phenomenon, and ways must therefore be sought of ensuring worker commitment. Labour turnover and absenteeism are similarly problems to which solutions must be sought. And at least the more enlightened managerial quarters recognise that older styles of unilateral decision-making are no longer adequate to deal with a more highly educated work force less habituated to conventional hierarchical structures.

These are some of the factors that account for the renewed interest in industrial democracy. However, many of the factors listed above have an obverse face, and there are other elements that effectively deflate such head of steam as may be building up.

Most obviously, there are vested interests that consciously or unconsciously oppose a greater spread of power at the workplace. The right of management and capital to take decisions unopposed is still vigorously defended, both ideologically and practically. The economic crisis has meant that the immediate safeguarding of employment and income levels overshadows other issues, which are postponed until smoother waters are reached. The growth of cartels and the concentration of economic power in the hands of fewer and fewer companies is a very apparent countervailing trend. Trade unionists are also afraid of taking on too much responsibility, whether for ideological reasons or because they simply do not have the resources to handle the problems posed by greater involvement in new areas of decision-making. It is a major goal of this chapter to assess how far education can contribute to overcoming these various obstacles.

It is necessary to add two further dimensions to this sketch of industrial democracy. First, industrial democracy can evolve at a number of levels. Tripartite discussions on economic strategy at the *national* level is one way in which new forms of decision-making can be introduced. In some countries, however, greater emphasis is placed on the *company* and on participation in corporate planning at this level. Yet the company – especially given the growth of conglomerates and multinationals – is often too large a unit for there to be much possibility of direct participation, and one must, therefore, also look to individual establishments within the company. Finally, there is the level of the work group. And cutting across these levels is the geographical dimension, demanding consideration of the impact of decisions on the region or the local community. It is important to bear in mind that the level at which decision-making powers are being shared obviously has a strong influence on the extent to which industrial democracy takes representative forms or allows more *direct* participation to occur.

Second, there is the question of how industrial democracy is introduced and promoted. There are basically two approaches here: *legislation* and *collective bargaining*. We refer to some of the relevant legislative measures in the next section, but it is obviously impossible to provide here a comprehensive catalogue of collective bargaining agreements. It is enough to point out that the existence of these two approaches means that one cannot judge the extent of industrial democracy in a given country simply by the presence or absence of legislation on the statute books. It is possible to say, though, that the four levels and the two approaches, in whatever permutations they appear, have differing implications for educational provision.

Finally, we offer some introductory remarks on the relationship of recurrent education to industrial democracy. Industrial democracy entails a capacity on the part of those involved to understand the processes of production and their various implications, and access to education is obviously a prerequisite for such understanding. Opening the company's books, for example, constitutes only a hollow gesture towards participation if the figures revealed have no significance except to those professionally trained in accountancy. Similarly, discussion of a firm's future investment policy depends for its coherence and value on those involved having some basic common economic language, hence the potential role for educational provision especially geared to the needs of adult workers.

Referring back to our crude three-stage scheme of developments in democracy, one can identify educational parallels. The introduction of political democracy was accompanied by the spread of compulsory education, aiming at an informed electorate capable of comprehending and deciding on political issues.

The evolution of the Welfare State powered by economic growth demanded more qualified manpower at all levels, and was, therefore, partly responsible for the explosion of post-secondary education and the development of a massive industrial training apparatus. If the suggestion of a third stage of democracy is at least plausible, the argument for policy thinking on the concomitant educational provision required is obvious. In contrast to the wealth of theorising and practical experience of schools, and the recent proliferation of studies on the relevance of adult education and training, there is a resounding silence on the subject of education for industrial democracy other than on the most general philosophical level such as the works of John Dewey. This paper aims simply at testing out the echoes.

2. *The Educational Dimension*

To speak of "education for industrial democracy" runs the risk of misleading in two ways. First, it may be understood as implying that the education involved is essentially preparatory, that it can be compared with initial training for a job or for the exercise of a particular set of defined skills. But conceptions and forms of industrial democracy are in a constant state of flux, and associated educational provision not only reflects that flux but is itself part of it. It cannot therefore be seen as a corpus of knowledge to be assimilated, nor even as a set of defined skills to be acquired, but rather as a continuing process which affects, and is affected by, changes in the distribution of power and in its socio-economic context.

The second point is closely associated. "Educational provision", "courses", "student" – all these are terms that automatically convey the image of a formalised learning process of the sort that prevails in most academic institutions. It is difficult to avoid using the educational vocabulary, so it is crucial to emphasize that the learning involved certainly does not need to take place physically in an academic environment nor does it need to be organised in the way that most education currently is.

This does not imply a rejection of structure in the learning process. Indeed, without some type of structure the notion of learning becomes vacuous, and all sorts of motivational problems arise. But if ever there was an issue that straddles the worlds of education and work, it is education for industrial democracy. Too ready an acceptance of existing educational forms would tilt the balance too far in one direction. In the longer term, the democratisation of work must have an impact on the organisation and control of the education system, and this is a theme to which we return later.

The aims of education for industrial democracy are necessarily as diverse and sometimes conflicting as the conceptions of industrial democracy itself. Two broad levels may be distinguished:

- At the macro level, one can analyse the role of education in general in promoting or hindering democracy, and *a fortiori* industrial democracy;

- At the micro level, one can look more closely at education that is more or less specifically geared to the equalisation of decision-making powers at the place of work.

The bulk of this analysis is concerned with the latter. However, it is worth reflecting on the more general effect of education. In the first place, rising overall levels of education have meant a growth in the aspirations of individuals, and have diminished their willingness to accept without question existing hierarchies and organisational patterns. This is most obviously the case for younger generations who have benefitted most from the quantitative expansion of post-secondary education. But it applies also to older people in two senses: they may have been able to exploit the increasing opportunities to return to some form of education or training and, more generally, they will have been affected by the overall spread of information and awareness about cultural and economic developments in their society.

How effectively the education system has contributed to this process is another question. Perhaps the major issue in this context is one that has been continually raised in relation to recurrent education more generally: what reforms are needed in initial education to provide a better basis for what comes later? It is worth underlining the fact, too, that many of the issues raised in the specific discussion of education for industrial democracy are relevant to the educational system in general, in terms of the role it plays in equipping people for participation in a democratic society. In this chapter, however, we focus on the specific issue of the links between recurrent education and industrial democracy.

a) *Organisation and Control*

One of the crucial issues involved in debates about recurrent education is whether or not a "parallel system" should develop, i.e. whether provision for returning adults should be made outside the mainstream or in some way integrated with it. The issue recurs if anything in more accentuated and complex form, in the case of education for industrial democracy.

Even the question "Should education for industrial democracy take place in a separate system?" may be premature. For perhaps the first issue to explore is the extent to which systematic provision is feasible. Of course, in every country there is management training and shop-steward or works councillor training, and in some cases this is fairly extensively developed and systematised. But how far are the existing structures capable of expanding and developing to cope with the new demands generated by the democratisation of work? Alternatively, how can one reasonably aim at building a systematic framework of educational provision?

This is a genuine question, and one that merits further consideration. It will certainly receive different answers from the different interested parties: management, trade unions, rank and file employees, governmental departments, and the providers themselves. For the moment, however, we proceed on the assumption that it is at least worth reflecting on the forms education could take, and that such reflections may lead to a clarification of the scope and desirability of systematic provision.

The Public Sector

In the debate on recurrent education, one of the arguments for developing separate provision for adults returning to education is that the formal system is not sufficiently adapted to respond to their particular needs, in terms of timing and location, educational content and teaching methods. All these arguments apply, if anything with added force, in the case of education for industrial democracy.

Trade union and labour movements traditionally prefer to establish and run their own provision on an independent basis. This is not so much because the public education system is perceived as being directly under managerial control as a reflection on the origins of the system itself. As the Swedish member of the CERI advisory group put it:

> The trade-union organisations are extremely dubious of the value of having active trade-union members go through the education previously restricted to representatives of the company. Often the experience is that established education affords a view and a language developed over a long period expressly to serve the hierarchical order of the economy they now want to change. The result would be not just unusable knowledge but also the risk of cooptation cooption? corruption?through the ideological thrust of the education. In order to come to terms with this type of difficulty, organisational changes are required that make education and knowledge acquisitions possible on a broad scale and in close contact with the practicalities with a democratic wage-earner perspective. No serious debate on this subject (let alone action) has yet got underway in the public education system.

Of the countries represented on the CERI group, the United Kingdom was virtually alone in the use made by the trade-union movement of institutions and tutors within the formal education sector, and even in that case there is a good deal of debate on the extent to which this is desirable and should continue. In North American countries, on the other hand, universities and colleges play a much more prominent part, with numerous schools of labour studies. The position in the United Kingdom was described as follows:

> While some courses involving union members are run by members of company training departments, and while a growing number of courses are run by the Trades Union Congress (TUC) and individual unions, the great bulk of courses are laid on by educational institutions who have also been concerned with the matter of control. Prior to the more active role of the TUC, courses were often largely determined by the academics and then agreed with the unions, and possibly employers, concerned. However, as the TUC began to play a more active role, it sought to lay down syllabuses, largely on the grounds that the unions were in the best situation to decide

75

what would be most useful for their workplace representatives. In addition, it would seem that there was a desire to ensure a minimum standard of education. Such a view conflicted with the liberal traditions within academia on a number of counts. For first it restricted the traditional right of the academic to determine course content; in other words, it conflicted with the notion of academic freedom.

Second, at least in some cases, courses for union activists were not solely aimed at training for the steward (or similar) role, but also sought to provide a broader education including a "second chance" to get on to, and climb, the educational ladder. A third possible factor was a difference in the sorts of horizons and approaches which were deemed desirable.

A traditional hostility, or at least mutual suspicion, between organised labour and education institutions is certainly a major factor. In some cases this is a straightforward ideological issue. In others, it is a recognition of the specific nature of trade unionists' learning needs, and the incapacity of teachers within the formal sector to adjust their training styles appropriately and, most importantly, to locate their teaching within a trade-union context. We return to this later.

Exceptions in other countries should be mentioned. Italy is unusual in that the growth of paid educational leave has largely relied on provisions in public schools and colleges paid for by the State within the system of "right to study". If this leave comes to be used for purposes of industrial democracy, a significant involvement of the public sector may develop. But this involvement has not so far extended to any of the education related to industrial democracy, which is exclusively union-based. In Germany, there have been one or two recent moves towards co-operation between unions and universities such as at Bochum, but in general, in spite of provisions for paid educational leave through legislation in a number of Lander and through collective agreements, very little is done by the public education sector to provide opportunities for training and education in industrial democracy problems and subjects. In France, there are several *Instituts de Travail,* publicly funded and attached to universities in which trade unionists follow advanced courses. These courses bring together leading officials from the different confederations, but they are concerned with broad political issues rather than with industrial democracy directly. In Norway, there is a new obligation on the public education sector to develop programmes for adults with work experience, although little of this is as yet related directly to industrial democracy.

However, there is not the total divide between the two systems there might appear to be. The public sector contribution should not be identified with the institutions alone. Individual teachers and professors can advise and teach trade unionists, and in many cases this is preferred by the labour organisations, since the choice of tutor remains with them. On the management side, the picture is very different. Extensive use is made of the public sector: many colleges and universities have specific departments of management studies, offering courses ranging from a short weekend to full-scale degrees, and consultancies abound. Moreover, evidence on paid educational leave points to managerial level employees enjoying greater opportunity both in the length of release and in the accepted scope of study. It is thus not surprising that both the French and the German reports to the CERI group comment that the disparity between the educational levels of management and labour is actually increasing.

The fact that it is impossible to assess the full extent of the public sector's contribution to management education is not due only to statistical inadequacies. There are many areas of study that may be relevant to management's needs, but it is not clear to what extent. Graduates from colleges or universities are likely to assume managerial posts and in a broad sense, therefore, the whole sector has at least a partial orientation, with managers operating from a much broader educational base. But it is obvious that, in varying degrees, the way subjects are structured is inevitably linked to the existing distribution of power and hence more closely geared to managerial interests than alternatives. Such codetermination appears to be accepted by the public sector more readily in the case of management than with trade unionists. This brings us back to the question of control, and we turn now to look at some of the issues raised as regards its distribution between management and labour.

Management and Labour: Separate Systems?

The question of control extends beyond the role of the public sector of education. In general, attitudes towards the control of education for industrial democracy reflect different conceptions of industrial democracy itself. A unitary perspective would insist on the need for joint training in order for management and labour to come to understand each other's problems more clearly. Even within this approach there are differences, essentially deriving from the extent to which the company insists on unilateral regulation of the joint courses. In other words, the joint appreciation and understanding of problems is at times to be developed within a teaching framework that is determined by only one of the participating groups.

In other instances, the training may be more democratically determined, and its organisation may itself be seen as a step towards greater participation. Management and unions sit down together and decide the content and structure of the courses. The state can also be involved. In Germany, for example, under the Enterprise Council Act of 1972, members of works councils have the right to paid leave of absence for up to three weeks during their period of office, and the training is recognised by the Lander Ministers of Labour after consultation with unions and employers.

Where joint regulation exists, a general consensus may indicate relatively equal positions and attitudes of mutual respect, but it may also represent marked inequalities, and the consensus is more a recognition of dominance or an acknowledgement of authority. In such cases, jointly determined educational provision will reinforce the inequalities.

In this respect, the submissions to the CERI group from France and Norway emphasize two different aspects of the same issue. The former raised a question which relates to training in general but also specifically to education for industrial democracy: "Training is intended to be the result of agreement between the sets of social groups concerned. But are employees really able to have their say since training has not modified the traditional distribution of power in that it has made the employer the financing and decision-taking partner in matters of training?". The problem of control is then located within the decision-making structure of enterprise:

> "Training activities will develop if concrete means of playing their role are effectively given to employee representatives. The development of training commissions, of *Comités d'Entreprise*, the presence of union representatives in the *Association de formation* (ASFO), the participation of union organisations in the management of training-insurance funds, will ensure a better participation by employees in the definition of training and thereby in the functioning of the enterprise."

However, the report notes a danger:

> "Many firms have created bigger and bigger training services which have the power to define, to evaluate in financial terms, and to control the firms' training activities. In their relations with these, employee representatives are distinctly at a disadvantage".

The paper from Norway looks from another perspective at the issue of whether or not representatives of management and labour not only share control of the organisation of education but actually participate in courses together. It sees this issue in terms of the distinction between theoretical training for industrial democracy, and – what is regarded as even more important in Norway – training in industrial democracy. Joint training is not expected to resolve all disagreement and conflict, but it is one of the ways in which, on the one hand, false divergences of interest can be revealed and, on the other, an agreement to disagree can be reached, presumably to mutual benefit.

In France and Italy, as one would expect given the ideological orientation of their unions, there is hardly any joint training for worker representatives and management. Norway has a more catholic approach which recognises the presence of conflicting interests yet looks for ways in which a dialogue can be initiated:

> Social learning, however, can best take place if groups with different interests are learning together. In such a learning process, they will have a chance to overcome the usual terminological and communication problems, and to dissolve some of the artificial disagreements which are based on ideologically influenced perceptions. Because of this, the Norwegian Employers' Confederation and the Norwegian Federation of Trade Unions have agreed to have both separate courses for owner representatives and employee representatives on the company board, and joint courses for both kinds of representatives from the same company. We do the same as regards the training of shop-stewards and management. We try to apply the same principle in all our learning activities. In courses for supervisors, we bring in the supervisors' superiors for periods of the course. We do the same for all courses for middle management.

The United Kingdom has perhaps the most highly variegated pattern of control over provision, and attitudes to control are similarly diverse. The report to the CERI group discusses a number of different patterns of control, all of which can be found in some companies, but:

> "It is clear that the debate over the control, and hence the structure, of steward and union education will continue, particularly at a general, rational level and given the role of the state in relation to legislation and financing. One other general point is also worthy of note: while there has been considerable debate over the control of union education, no such pressure has existed to challenge unilateral employer control over management education, given in relation to consciously democratic systems, despite the much greater state funding than for union education."

In the United Kingdom, there are some in-company courses that bring together management and employees, but official union policy is clearly opposed to such courses being held where they deal directly with issues surrounding bargaining, industrial relations, and worker representation. It is very rare to find union courses that include managers – other than where they themselves are union members.

The growing unionisation of managerial employees has blurred the line dividing management from the rest of the workforce, an issue reflected in the debate concerning the German 1976 Codetermination Act which includes a management representative on the workers' side. Managers who are union members therefore frequently participate in courses alongside shop-floor members. Managers certainly have their own separate educational provision. There is a wide range of educational and training efforts by employers' associations, by companies (increasingly at this level) and by private institutions, to provide managers with training for the handling of matters under the Enterprise Council Act of 1972 and the Codetermination Act of 1976, especially in the field of personnel management, the handling of wages systems, and of plant or job layout.

Some management education can be identified as directly related to industrial democracy, but the content varies greatly. Some courses cover broad industrial relations questions while others aim to encourage participative styles of management and better communication. The introduction of autonomous work groups has sometimes been accompanied by courses for managers in the underlying philosophy and the implications for their roles. Developments in modern management theory may have caused some changes in concepts of management so that it may be seen formally as involving a far greater number of employees. But it is a moot point how far that change is reflected in the philosophy and practice of management education.

This matter of control over education cannot, however, be resolved simply in terms of whether or not separate systems exist. Questions need to be raised about what sort of systematic provision is to be aimed for, by unions, management, and public authorities, but such provision has to be made in a given climate of industrial relations, which changes both over time and within and between companies. Decisions on the structure of provision will, therefore, inevitably be affected by each party's judgement on the resources at its disposal (both currently and in the foreseeable future), and on the extent to which it can aim for a uniform system.

One final speculative question can be raised in this context. How far is education playing a part in a zero-sum game as far as the distribution of power is concerned? If one party equips itself well educationally, does this automatically mean that the others fall back? Or is it possible that both sides learn how to press their cases, which may conflict or may coincide, although overall extent of control is expanded, as a general rule, by improved effectiveness and quality of the skills of the participants?

Trade-union education: Confederal or decentralised?

In some countries it is relatively easy to envisage a coherent and fairly homogeneous system of trade-union education that reflects the overall nature of trade-union organisation – Germany and the Scandinavian countries provide the obvious examples. In these countries there is a relatively structured progression, from basic to advanced courses. The basic courses are provided locally, if possible, often at the workplace itself, as in the case of the Scandinavian study circles. The circles operate for two hours a week, and normally run for a total of twenty to forty hours. The next step is a longer course organised on a regional basis, while the most advanced courses are provided centrally. A roughly similar progression operates in Germany. There is, perhaps, a stronger emphasis on the industrial sector, with each of the major industrial unions running its own system. The central confederation, the DGB, helps smaller unions which do not have the resources to develop their own system, and puts on courses that are so advanced as to be uneconomic for individual unions to mount them on their own.

Even in these countries, however, there are divisions which inhibit the development of a single unified system – in Sweden, blue-collar and white-collar unionists are trained separately by their respective organisations, the LO and the TCO. The division between manual and non-manual grades is only one dimension. The divisions between different industries, between different unions (whether or not they are in the same industry or industries) and between different levels of organisation are also important.

In both France and Italy, the different confederations do not combine, but maintain their verging political viewpoints. In France, moreover, the CGT (Confédération générale du travail) and CFDT (Confédération françise et démocratique du travail) hold different attitudes towards centralisation. This results in the former operating a more highly centralised system, while the latter provides only a basic political framework and leaves the rest to its regional organisation. In Italy, the main division is between activities organised by the confederations and those organised by the leading sectors such as the metalworkers.

Both of these are chiefly carried out centrally, but one confederation at least – the CGIL – is studying the possibility of decentralising initiatives. This means combining different levels of union education, and planning training for rank and file together with that of officials at plant level to develop a *vertical process* of educational support for industrial democracy. In the United Kingdom, some unions choose to operate their own system of education, while others rely exclusively on the TUC.

In short, the organisation of union education is highly differentiated along the dimensions of, on the one hand, centralised versus decentralised and, on the other hand, confederal versus single sector or single union. The obvious question is what permutation or permutations are most appropriate in any given context and why?

b) *Process and Content*

This chapter has placed special emphasis on the need for education to be oriented towards solving problems rather than learning facts or objectives. The aim is not to produce people who are highly knowledgeable in the abstract, but capable of applying what they learn, of translating it into action. Taken literally, the phrase "problem solving" implies a process with a more or less defined end in view – the problem has been "solved" (or accepted as "insoluble"). But the solving of a given problem does not, of course, automatically lead to a state of peaceful equilibrium. If anything, the reverse is true, for the raising and exploration of that problem is more likely to expose other, more fundamental problems. Once the process has started, it sets up a dynamic of its own, as is described in the Norwegian report:

> Education makes you conscious of the lack of influence on your own life and work surroundings. It creates a kind of dissatisfaction which is necessary for all development. If this dissatisfaction is not to lead to aggression and frustration, it needs to be supplemented with education which may help in the process of finding better solutions. Democratisation can be said to be a process of "education – dissatisfaction – problem-solving and solution – more education – new dissatisfaction – problem-solving and solution".

The process, therefore, resembles a spiral, raising both competence and aspirations. In other words, workers who had previously been excluded from the process of defining problems come to have a say in it, and consequently issues and areas which had been regarded as non-problematic become subject to debate and negotiation.

Individual and collective learning

The French report observes that the priority given to problem-solving is shared between education for industrial democracy and recent reforms in initial schooling; both demonstrate a shift towards a more active, project-centred approach. But in schools, problem-solving and project-based learning tends to be a way of allowing the individual to pursue his or her own interests, as opposed to a uniform class activity. By contrast, the types of problems which arise under industrial democracy relate to groups of people, rather than single individuals. Moreover, the learning that occurs in the solving of problems is very much a group activity, especially since it concerns people who are, on the whole, accustomed, at the workplace, to functioning in groups and who rely on the mutual support that this allows. So, one could, perhaps, suggest that it is the collective definition and the collective solution of problems with which education for industrial democracy is concerned, and this distinguishes it markedly from progressive school methods, on the one hand, and from orthodox higher education and research on the other.

The Swedish study circle is well known for the contribution it has made to adult education in general. Although study circles originated with the temperance movement and traditionally aimed at improving the individual's diligence and good habits, they are potentially well suited to a different style, offering a simple forum in which to raise general questions in a tangible context and a chance to learn from the experience of others.

A problem-solving approach is intended to increase the relevance of education and overcome the lack of motivation on the part of many working people. But this leads us back to the potential conflict between collective and individual learning objectives. One goal of educational policy generally has been to provide opportunities for people to improve their social and economic position, and it has, therefore, been closely linked to mobility on the labour market. This was part of a relatively optimistic growth philosophy which envisaged a continuing expansion of better jobs and a demand for more highly qualified personnel that would be accompanied by an increased supply of people who had taken the opportunity to acquire more skills and qualifications. The breakdown of this optimism can be seen to have had profound effects on people's view of education.

Instead of a reliance on individuals acquiring new skills in response to change, there is an increasing awareness that the nature of many modern changes demands a collective response, such as the production of alternative plans for restructuring industry. Education then becomes a means of developing such a collective strategy in order to resolve personal and group problems. The shift is from education as a means of enhancing individual mobility to education as a means of increasing collective stability. The link with decision-making and democracy is clear: rather than individuals accepting decisions made by the providers of employment and adapting themselves accordingly, they are seeking to influence these decisions so that the burden of adjustment does not fall on them alone. Equally clearly, the definition of a problem as a collective, not as an individual one, calls for revised ideas on what sort of education is appropriate.

The conventional orientation of education emphasizes social and professional mobility, based on the ethos of personal competition. The growth of participation may entail a change of attitudes amongst adult learners: without prejudice to the desire to excel, they may come more to seek to achieve their objectives through co-operation in work and study. Under such circumstances, the drive to distance oneself from one's fellows in terms of personal performance may, to some extent, be replaced by the wish to contribute to common goals. This does not imply a denial that individual talents and tastes may differ, nor does it suggest that conflict, either between groups or between individuals will disappear. The argument is quite simply that the process of democratic decision-making is likely to put a much higher premium on the collective definition of problems and a co-operative approach to their resolution. Education may contribute to this by tapping the creative potential of the work force as a whole, even though the creativity may not always be directed towards traditional objectives.

The relevance of occupational training

How far is education for industrial democracy a separate process from occupational training? At first sight, they may appear to be wholly independent of each other, but to treat the two in total isolation would ignore important trends in the demand for skills and their application to the workplace. On the one hand, industrial democracy is concerned to advance the ability of working people to exercise control over their working lives; on the other hand, the increasing division of labour, progressive specialisation, and the concomitant (if uneven) process of deskilling combine to diminish that ability. As the Swedish report puts it: "a crucial point, particularly as concerns the vertical division of labour, is that the workers not only lose control for the moment over the work they do, but above all lose the chance to retain and cultivate their occupational skill. This means that they can be replaced more easily, and thus their position in production also weakens."

We questioned above whether continuing overall growth in the demand for educated labour can still be assumed. If, instead, the pattern of demand has become frozen or static, this may lead to a polarisation between a small number of jobs requiring highly educated workers and a growing number of unskilled, dead-end occupations. This would have implications for industrial democracy and its educational provision. First, there is the argument that the diminution of opportunities for exercising skills on the job can and should be balanced by an increase in the opportunities for participating in decisions at the workplace. What this envisages is essentially a trade-off: less scope for responsibility and initiative in one sector of working life compensated for by more scope in another.

A less fatalistic argument might suggest that the response to the threatened polarisation of skills should not be to accept it and compensate for it, but to combat it by challenging its inevitability. The educational process should consequently begin before decisions that determine the content of jobs are taken, and should aim to influence these decisions and ensure that the jobs themselves are satisfying. In other words, working life should offer people the opportunity to develop and exercise a variety of skills, relating both to the technical performance of their job and to decisions on its organisation and structure.

These two lines of thought are not, however, mutually exclusive. For decisions may be taken democratically which nevertheless entail – for example, for reasons of efficiency or competitiveness – the existence of jobs that are intrinsically without interest or challenge. In these cases, the notion of compensation via participation would apply – the important feature being that the way in which this policy is developed is itself democratic.

The link with the theme of individual versus collective learning can now be made more explicit. Through group work it is possible not only to retain some latitude in the job assigned but also to regain and maintain greater control of the work within the individual group. In Sweden LO has group-organised work as a main point in its programme for industrial democracy. Such a programme could mean that in education, in a different sense from its traditional organisation and connotation, the individual will have to be prepared to work in groups.

For the education system, this may well mean increased demands upon basic occupational education and its future development. If extreme specialisation in the division of labour is to be stopped, greater allowance must be made for occupational training and expertise. This implies that occupational education should be conducted in larger units, in which people are trained not only in certain on-the-job motions but also in fundamental principles of technology and its intrinsic promise and risk.

Similarly, at the secondary level, preparation for participation in working life should not be conceived of only in terms of technical skills, however broad their application. Such skills should be integrated into an education that prepares young people for full participation in the functioning of an enterprise.

The definition of the scope of workers' occupational training, therefore, reflects the degree of control they are expected to exercise over their work. On the one hand, they can be trained to carry out jobs that have been conceived and defined by others, and are given no opportunity to understand their place in the production process. On the other hand, they can acquire the fundamental occupational competence that forms the basis for active participation and responsibility for the organisation of production.

Content: Procedural Versus Substantive, and
Technical Versus Political

The theme of the previous section was that education for industrial democracy is, in many respects, closely inter-related with occupational training. This was seen to be particularly true in relation to the development of autonomous work groups, and, at this level, it is the participatory rather than the representative conception of industrial democracy which dominates. We turn now to look more at the educational implications of *representation* and the training involved.

It would be fruitless to recite detailed lists of the content of education for worker representatives in the different countries. Much of the learning that takes place is informal, and derives from a process of mutual exchange of views and information, and even on formal courses, the syllabus may give relatively little genuine insight into what is actually learnt. Nevertheless, different types of education may be distinguished according to various criteria, which may be represented as opposite points on a spectrum. For example, is the education basically aimed at familiarising the student with the rules according to which the democratic process takes place, or with the content of the issues on which decisions are being made? This can be treated as a procedural/substantive spectrum.

There are often considerable differences in the emphasis given to the goal of helping a representative to concentrate on improving his understanding of how to enter into consultation or negotiation and his ability to follow the union rule book (procedural), as compared with his direct understanding of the subjects under discussion (substantive). Similarly, a manager may learn more about how to devise and implement a participation scheme or about the actual substance of the decisions to be reached under such schemes. Inevitably, however, skill in operating or manipulating the procedure will greatly affect the substance of the decisions.

Just as it is possible to envisage a procedural/substantive spectrum, there may exist a technical/political spectrum, relating to how things are done and decisions taken. A purely technical approach to training in enterprise manpower policy, for example, would focus predominantly on issues such as labour turnover and manning levels, viewed essentially in relation to the functioning of the enterprise as a separate and specific entity. One would expect a more democratically managed enterprise to take greater account of the interests of all employees than one run on traditional grounds, but this could still be restricted to a relatively technical analysis. The other end of the spectrum, by contrast, would cover more fundamental issues such as the accumulation of capital and the overall tendency of the rate of profit. These would for instance be related to the employment implications of changes in the labour/capital ratio. It would have to be less exclusively concerned with the functioning of the particular enterprise, and more broadly concerned with national or international trends and issues.

Education for industrial democracy can embrace both highly technical and highly political perspectives. Representatives involved in democratic decision-making can learn both how enterprises are currently run and how these techniques might be adapted and modified, and also what the surrounding environment is like and what the basic political issues are.

The mix of these perspectives may thus be crucial. In the case of Germany, some of the highly politicised training appears to be ineffectual because, for various reasons, its relevance to workplace issues is not appreciated:

> While there is in many cases – though definitely not in all – a fairly leftist and in many cases definite Marxist base of philosophy in teaching on general political and socio-economic affairs, the outlook on actual problems of the enterprise, the plant

or collective bargaining is fairly consistent with a capitalist system prevailing in West Germany. A leftist and radical thought is frequently counteracted by very pragmatic approaches to industrial and shop-floor problems.

It could be argued that the "problems" can only be tackled via the full-blooded political analysis of the economic and social system, yet this seems to clash with the difficulty representatives have in applying such analysis to daily life on the shop-floor. Differences in defining the problems occur not only between management and labour, but also among those within labour and within management who take different views on the context within which the problems are to be located.

Broadly speaking, it would appear that in France and Italy, training is heavily weighted towards the political side, though in the latter case the unions seem to be shifting slightly in their orientation and taking the view that there is also a need to participate in and learn about techniques of managing an enterprise within the existing system, albeit with strong reservations. In France, the union attitude is very much that there must be a major social and economic change as a pre-condition for the establishment of industrial democracy – and even then there are doubts as to whether unions should participate in the rnning of enterprises. Certain trade unions in France, particularly the *Connfédération française et démocratique du Travail* (CFDT), seek explicitly wider social change through self-management practices in all areas of social life, both professional and non-professional. The French report notes, however, that training is not considered as a major instrument for introducing self-management social practices of this type.

The ambivalent and changing union attitude is described in the Italian report in terms of a "two-sided" model which:

- On the one hand, has emphasized the "dispute aspect", that of confrontation at the level of the productive unit and the employers' side, within a 'political' perspective (i.e. the union as the exponent of alternative 'models' of society);
- On the other hand, has simultaneously supported the development of a consulting role, on regular subjects of major decisions concerning economic policy, within the customary triangle: public (central and/or local) power-employers-unions.

In particular, the latter aspect of the model has been developed to such an extent that the union is now present in the institutions which are responsible for many interventions in the economic and social field. This has contributed to the development of a union approach:

- Increasingly favourable to democratic control of the economy conducted at the level of relations with public power, at times of major economic decisions;
- Reluctant, however, to face up to the realities of the enterprise which require a modification of those attitudes that refer exclusively to a "culture of confrontation". This ambivalence is reflected in the discussion on educational provision.

The German case is interesting, because there is a tendency towards division of labour, with some of the technical decisions being left to experts, with worker representatives dealing with more basic issues. Apparently, while there has been a strong emphasis on the part of certain professionals to teach certain business administration subjects (for example, analysis of balance sheets in a very technical sense), there is nowadays a tendency to give more weight to work-oriented questions and concepts and to leave the interpretation of balance sheets and the like to the experts and professionals. There is an increasing stress on the development of information systems and company indicators within the enterprise, in co-operation with the works council members of the plants concerned. The implications of basic business and investment decisions on personnel structure and quantity play a dominant role.

In the United Kingdom, training for worker representation used to be clearly situated towards the procedural and technical ends of the spectrum. This may now be changing though there is far less of a clear and agreed political perspective than in the previous cases. It has been observed that the TUC, in particular, is moving towards syllabuses that raise questions and broader issues than the mechanics of payment systems, etc. This is particularly true in the area of industrial democracy, where the emphasis now is less upon the debate surrounding the issue of worker directors than the best ways in which worker influence can be extended, including extending union membership.

Judging from the reports, the syllabuses used in Norway and Sweden come the nearest to a combination of the political and technical, though this approach itself reflects certain political attitudes. Thus, there can be a reorganisation of major issues and disagreements surrounding the nature of the relationship between labour and capital, without that necessarily discouraging worker representatives from acquiring the skills needed to influence in detail managerial decisions on a long-term planning basis.

Democracy Within Education

If the education is to be action-oriented and relevant to the concrete problems of the students, it is not mere rhetoric to argue that they themselves should participate in the elaboration of their own programme of study. The question is how far is this possible in practical terms, and what means can be used to enable them to articulate and define their own problems? The principle of democratising the learning process is obviously desirable, but there is an element of circularity: those who are fully able to articulate their learning needs are half way to the solution already.

The Norwegians have given legal recognition to the belief that a certain degree of self-management has a positive effect on adult learning. The Adult Education Act of 1976 requires all organisations that receive public support for adult education to adopt democratic principles with substantial influence exercised by the participants: "organisations and institutions which are accepted (for financial support) are required to give the participants in the courses opportunities to influence both the content and the administration of the course". Signifi-

the same principles apply to internal company training if it is to qualify for financial support.

The difficulty of implementing self-management of the educational process is compounded, paradoxically, by the expectations of the learners themselves. They are accustomed to learning organised in schools, with the transmission of knowledge as the central objective and the teacher as the repository of wisdom. Their judgement of a successful course tends to be a quantitative one, based on the amount of information accumulated and even on the physical bulk of factual documents.

Learning to organise one's own study is an important skill which must be gradually developed. There can be no general rule as to how to break into the circle described above. But to focus attention on this principle is one way of reinforcing the argument for the principle of recurrent education, for it is often only towards the end of a study period that the participant begins to be able to define more clearly what his or her future learning needs are – and this process repeats itself. It is, therefore, essential that education for industrial democracy is not seen as basically preparatory, but as a recurring process.

The definition of need is therefore problematic, and we return to it later in our discussion of the role of professionals. Associated with this, however, is an equally thorny problem: how to judge to what extent these needs have been satisfactorily met. The more education is related to events on the shop floor, the more difficult it becomes to isolate and define its contribution. The report from Norway puts it in the following way:

> In companies, many projects have been started with a double purpose. Usually there is a problem to be solved, a solution to be found, or a system to be developed. In addition, the process itself is planned in such a way as to have a maximum learning effect. Such programmes are, therefore, clearly problem-oriented, the training is informal, and the subject learning may cover several fields and come in only as a help in finding the solution or solving the problem. This is not what is usually termed "education". It is a learning process of a social nature and subject learning is only a means to an end. Consequently, it is difficult, if not impossible, to evaluate the results as regards knowledge.

The notion of evaluation is particularly elusive. Some systematic attempts are made, but the United Kingdom report, which itemises various techniques that have been tried, goes on to point out the difficulties involved:

> Changes in action may occur only some time after the course, as particular events and opportunities arise. Similarly, while the TUC may have certain objectives, at the same time syllabuses are designed to foster mutual education among students....The possibility that TUC and student objectives may differ clearly complicates evaluation ... Evaluation is made additionally difficult by the conflicting goals that are frequently to be found and reflect the differing notions and aims of industrial democracy.

Communication skills

A further characteristic of education for industrial democracy is its concern with developing the ability of participants to communicate with each other and with those they represent – their "constituents". Indeed, for some parties – most particularly the employers – communication is largely what industrial democracy is all about. For example, the Confederation of British Industry, the United Kingdom employers' organisation, has christened the department responsible for its work on industrial democracy and participation the "Employee Communications Unit", and its educational message is that channels of communication between the different hierarchical levels need to be unblocked and broadened. In some other countries, many of the participation schemes are not designed to include decision-making, but have as their explicit remit the improvement of information flows – there is some difference of emphasis on how far the flows are two-way, from shop floor to management as well as top downwards.

But the concern with communications is by no means the exclusive concern of management, and does not always accompany the somewhat restricted concept of industrial democracy described above. On the labour side, there are two main aspects: communications between central and local levels, and between the representative and his/her constituents. In Italy, one of the two general objectives identified for union training is to enable the student to relay the results of participation to all workers. Some Italian union leaders (CGIL, for example) have actually spoken of a training module having *diffuse responsibilities* and others (CISL) have referred to a newly emerging role, that of *training agent*. Of growing cncern, however, is the risk of creating a sort of union "super official" detached from the rank and file even more than is already the case.

These dangers and some possible solutions can be summarised as follows:

Dangers	Remedies
– The official becomes too technical	– In training, a "union", not merely a technical, viewpoint must be maintained
– The official becomes detached from the rank and file	– He/she must be given a function which is both involved with training and with diffusion of information.

The same lesson has been derived in Germany where, over the last few years, many unions and workers' representatives on boards especially noticed that communication poses major problems. Since their role on the boards has to respect the interests of the companies and frequently has to keep essential information confidential, little space is left for manoeuvering on the workers' side. The danger of a real separation between the representatives and the represented may become acute. During the last few years, therefore, the role of training in proper expression and language as well as in discussion and negotiation techniques has increased.

There is no doubt that this is a priority in the United Kingdom as well, at several levels. Training for newly appointed worker directors in the Post Office was heavily preoccupied with developing communication skills; at the other end of the spectrum, shop-stewards attempting to conduct collective bargaining in new areas, i.e. outside traditional pay and conditions, repeatedly acknowledge the difficulties they have in convincing their members of the significance and relevance of decisions in these areas. Oddly enough, in earlier years – the Black Ages of trade-union education – one of the few courses available for unionists was actually on elocution (not that effective communication is to be identified with proper enunciation).

The Scandinavian study circle is, of course, not primarily concerned with industrial democracy but is, perhaps, the prime example of a policy intended to provide mass basic education and thus further a broad understanding of the issues to be decided. These circles may not concern themselves directly with developing communication skills, but in the case of trade-union circles their deliberate if indirect effect is to facilitate the process of communication between officials and the rank and file. Study circle leaders are trained in the use of the (centrally provided) materials, and this training can itself be seen as part of that process. There are strict obligations imposed in Sweden on representatives at higher levels to report back competently; while in Norway, the whole ethos of participation means that, in principle at least, there is widespread concern with keeping constituents informed.

c) *Learning Resources*

New technology has, of course, opened up enormous possibilities for improving availability of information and the development of teaching programmes, but we concentrate here essentially on human resources and the potential contributions of different groups: tutors, researchers, professionals, experts, and the participants themselves.

Our earlier discussion of the organisation of education for industrial democracy included the place of the public educational sector and some of the reasons for its rather peripheral role at present. There are five major factors which tend to reduce the value of conventional academics for our subject. First, they are accustomed to thinking and teaching within single disciplines, a style which does not easily accommodate itself to a problem-solving approach. Second, their students are characteristically young and with a relatively successful educational record, whereas many of those participating in education for industrial democracy will lack formal education and the learning habits of a young student. Third, they tend to put great weight on the acquisition of information, often involving the analysis and digestion of large amounts of textual material. Fourth, they often lack direct experience of industry and even of contact with working people. Finally — and perhaps most critically — the notion of academic freedom may reduce their commitment ot mett the learning needs of particular groupe where there is a strong orientation towards action.

As to the potential contribution of the academic community, we must start, of course, by admitting the openness of the debate on the appropriate way of teaching adults. The difficulties here experienced by the academic are, to some extent, compounded by the nature of the groups concerned with industrial democracy. Experience of training adults has been accumulating, it is true, but the French report strikes a juduciously critical note about the difference between abstract knowledge and practical capabilities, and reminds us that listening to talk is not the same as learning how to love. "Is it not a myth to suggest that what had been the norm for 10 to 15 years of schooling, that is, learning how to live by hearing abour life, could suddenly be transformed within the space of 5 to 10 days of residential seminars in a country hotel?"

At the least we can say that some of the difficulties are recognised in principle. The altered role of the teacher is put succinctly in the Norwegian report:

> In problem-oriented project work, the role of the "trainer" is different from in a traditional educational situation. The main task for the trainer is to create a social situation where all the participants can mobilise their knowledge and insight related to the problem they are to solve. The trainer must also helt to furnish the group with outside specialised knowledge when this is needed. His main task is consequently not to 'teach', but to guide the process so that it gives the participants a maximum experience of how to use the collective knowledge in the group for a common purpose.

Translation of the principle into practice is probably a long way off in most countries. The question thus arises of where one should look for teachers who have the apprpriate combination of experience, pedagogical skills and political awareness? The conventional source for students — training colleges, catering largely for students coming more or less straight from school — is patently inappropriate. The adequacy of *ad hoc* sources is likely to be severely strained if there is a significant expansion of various forms or industrial democracy with their accompanying training demands. One is led one step further back to the question of who, if anyone, is to train the teachers, and this harks back to what we have already said about organisation and control, and the question of how far systamtisaion is necessary or desirable.

One way of relieving the pressure on tutors is to employ outsiders with particular expertise. This is a trend likely do develop rapidly in response both to the quantitative pressures referred to earlier and to the problem of areas to be covered. However, the same problems recur with regard to these specialists: in areas like accountancy, it seems that it has been particularly difficult to find people who combine the requiste specialist skills a sympathy with unions, and an ability to adopt the traditional and valued role of the union tutor. There are two main aspects: the *attitude* of the "expert" and the *nature* of his or her "expertise".

The first is essentially the same problem as that which confronts adult education in general, but rendered more acute by the fact that the "expert" will probably have had less time to reflect specifically on the learning needs of adult students, and will also be more committed to the status of a particular field of expertise.

The "professionals" in this connection are the educators, the teachers within the public education sector and the training personnel within organisations and companies. Irrespective of their professional background and training, they have the same plattern of education, which is the traditional role of the teacher in the clasroom, the teacher *who knows* and the children who do not know. The situaiton in adult education is quite different. First, the participants must be regarded as highly motivated people with a certain amount of knowledge and experience, people who do not want ti learn for the sake of mastering a subject, but who want to learn how to use their knowledge and experience in solving a problem. Second, this change in attitude must be followed by learning new training methods, mainly how to plan and guide a social process of co-operative learning.

One objective of education for industrial democracy is to build up the confidence of participants, particularly those who have little formal education. In many cases, workers are confronted with an unfamiliar setting, unfamiliar procedures, and unfamiliar language, and it its extremely difficult for them to establish their presence effectively. Board-room discussions, for example, take place against a background which is, for social and historical reasons, infinitely more suited do directors than to worker representatives. In part, this is a matter of social convention. Other differences, however, are rooted in the origins and functions of existing managerial practice: the language of accountancy, for instance, derives from assumptions about profit and loss which are often at odds with the notion that workers who invest their labour in an enterprise have at least equal rights with shareholders who invest their capital.

Education can serve to mobilise the potential of those who are often demoralised by professional obscurantism, and this mobilisation often occurs via co-operation with fellow learners. A major resource is, thus, the participants themselves. We have already stressed the importnace of the informal exchange of ideas and information, and the danger that a systemisation of eductional provision may stifle thos process. The question that arises is, nevertheless, how best to tap practical knowledge and experience so that it can multiply and spread. In the United Kingdom, there are centres organised by shop-stewards and often aided by local unions, though not necessarily recognised by the TUC, which provide advice and support to workers on issues such as health and safety. Additionally, there are resource centres which place the emphasis on mutual education and study involving both academics and trade unionists, often in long term investigations of their industries or companies with the possible aim of developing alternative corporate plans.

But the focus here is not so much on organisations as on the people themselves, and this raises the important issue of the composition of the student body. How far can employees from different industries, from different unions, from public and private sectors, from different grades, learn from each other? Of particular interest is the extent to which blue and white collar workers learn together. The historical divide between the two is most graphically evident in Sweden with the clear-cut separation between the LO and TCO. (There is an equivalent divide in Norway which is reinforced in both cases by the blue-collar organisation's official ties with the political labour or social democrat parties). In Germany, union representatives from the managerial ranks are in a highly ambiguous position, but this has not meant a complete separation:

> While trade-union training for works council members reflects, statistically speaking, the composition of this group (with a predominance of skilled workers and qualified white-collar personnel), under the existing laws blue-collar and white-collar employees both must be represented on boards of companies. In many cases, the occupational knowledge and expertise of many white-collar employees prove to be a very important aid in the internal preparation of board meetings amongst the workers' representatives.

For educational purposes, there are considerable advantages in segregation. It is easier to relate the teaching and educational materials to specific problems if students share a common industrial background, which can otherwise be difficult when representatives from manual grades in the private sector are sitting alongside those from white-collar grades in the public administration. On the other hand, to segregate provision reinforces these divisions, and increases the likelihood of sectional groups pursuing their own interests exclusively, without having the opportunity of understanding the outlook of others.

One of the most frequently recognised benefits of mixed courses is that they are an almost unique occasion for the participants to find out what happens in other industries, what problems they have in common with employees from other sectors, and so on. Often this derives from discussion outside the formal educational setting, where participants exchange information and ideas naturally and establish a network of contacts which can be one of the major lasting benefits of a course. Segregated provision makes it more difficult for people moving from one occupational sector to another to adapt, especially if they assume representative functions. The basic concept of solidarity may also militate in favour of bringing workers together to study alongside one another. In brief, the role of education in bridging (or alternatively broadening) gaps between different employee groups merits detailed observation.

All the agents mentioned – academic researchers, tutors, professionals of various kinds, representatives, and shop-floor workers – have contributions to make. The problem is to see how these different contributions complement each other, and to learn more about the relative values of the various permutations. One could, in conclusion, suggest that the process of continuing negotiation of teaching and learning, should contain three essential elements of education for industrial democracy:

- Confrontation of different interested parties, with or without eventual reconciliation;
- Mutuality between teacher and learner;
- Continuous change, i.e. recognition of the time dimension.

3. *Issues for Further Consideration*

We have examined some of the themes that could constitute the basis for a debate on the role of education in industrial democracy, although as we stressed at the outset, the debate is very much in its infancy. It seems, therefore, worthwhile to suggest some further lines along which the subject – education for industrial democracy – may be explored in research.

a) *Methodology*

The key issue here concerns the ways in which the research itself can and should be organised so as to contribute to the educational process, and who is to be involved in the learning that takes place. What are the rights of those who are the "objects" of research, in terms of their participation in it and their access to the results? In this respect, one of the regulations for the award of grants from the Norwegian Department of Municipal and Works Affairs is worth quoting: "We will give priority to projects which are oriented towards practical application and where communication and use of the results are part of the projects. In this connection, we will stress that the researchers have direct contact with the field and that those who are influenced by the research results are taking part in the research from the very start". This is not to suggest that all research must be action-oriented. But the *relationship between researcher and researched* is worth reflecting on, however directly or indirectly it is tied in to a process of change.

We have already stressed that flux and instability are dominant characteristics of the contemporary context for industrial democracy. Therefore, the control of variables, so central to the principle of laboratory experimentation, is simply not feasible. Nor, indeed, can the consequences and the outcome of the research itself be controlled. Even if the goal is the straightforward accumulation of knowledge, this takes place against a shifting social and industrial background, with literally unpredictable consequences. The same is true of action research to an even greater extent.

In brief, the problem of methodology can be tied very directly to our central concern by posing the question: how far is research itself to be conceived of as an educational process? And this question need not be confined to the span of the individual research project itself, for it contains within it the germs of another: how far, and in what ways, can people in the field be helped to conceive and carry out their own research?

b) *Structure and organisation*

The lack of empirical material from this problem area is evident. The first plea under this heading, therefore, is for the development of a fuller picture of how education for industrial democracy is provided at present, and who controls and administers it. But such a line of research needs to be taken further with an analysis of the way provision is organised. The degree to which systematic provision is either feasible or desirable is an issue we have discussed under the heading "The Educational Dimension"; this could be pursued in order to reveal what sort of managerial approaches are used and how appropriate they are.

The role of the public sector, and national policy on it, also deserves close scrutiny. But there is also a strong geographical dimension to this. The way in which local or regional educational resources are mobilised is of obvious relevance. Conversely, the extent to which education for industrial democracy is geared to meet the needs of the local community is equally important. If, for example, there is less emphasis placed on individual mobility and more on a collective approach to the solution of common problems, what are the implications for the planning and organisation of local or regional educational policies? This brings us back again to the question of power: who is to control the allocation and use of resources in this context?

Similar issues within the company merit attention. To what extent can and should education for industrial democracy be a jointly-managed operation and what are the implications for the existing machinery of participation and negotiation? Can this be separated from the development of company training policy in general, given the arguments we have already advanced for a close association between occupational training and education for industrial democracy?

We turn finally to what happens within the education, to its internal management. Stress has already been laid on the need to search for new and democratic ways of defining the curriculum and organising the learning process. What are the implications for teachers, whether formally qualified or not? From where should the teaching personnel be drawn, and should they be primarily concerned with facilitating the exchange of information between students or should they have a more direct contribution to make? Lying behind this is an attitudinal problem: how far are those who come to learn themselves prepared to take on the task of organising their own education?

c) *Group and individual learning*

We have paid a good deal of attention to the impetus industrial democracy may give to the notion of group or collective learning, as distinct from the highly individualised emphasis of most current educational modes. Indeed, the shift towards a more collective view of education is rated in the Swedish report as the most important implication of industrial democracy for educational policy.

There is obvious scope for fundamental research into the processes of collective learning. What sorts of skills do members of the group need in order to participate effectively in such a process, and how do these differ from those associated with learning on an individual basis? How are they related to actual work processes? What are the implications for teaching styles and teaching materials? Which areas of study are most amenable to some sort of collective approach, and which are more suitably tackled on an individual basis?

The definition of groups, and the way this will vary in different circumstances, is a further potential subject of study, especially from an empirical point of view. For example, it would be interesting to investigate how far supervisors or junior management can come together with middle or senior management in a joint approach to solving problems.

Streaming, or the extent to which diversity of aptitude and attainment is manageable within a group, is a highly contentious subject as far as schools are concerned. The same subject is relevant to education for industrial democracy, although, perhaps, not quite so controversial. The more that different groups of employees are brought into decision-making, and educational provision for them is recognised as necessary, the more this problem will assume prominence and need study. Is it possible and desirable to define a minimum level of educational attainment? Can successive levels be satisfactorily differentiated? What sort of balance or trade-off is there between formal education and work experience? To what extent is a common industrial background necessary? These questions are difficult enough in themselves, but they are likely also to receive different answers according to the particular area at which the education is aimed.

Finally, under this heading comes the question of size, in particular the implications of the size of the enterprise for the organisation of the learning groups. For instance, how far does a giant conglomerate dictate a different composition of student groups from that which may be appropriate to a small enterprise? It is highly improbable that there can be a single model, and comparative studies could help to uncover some of the more influential factors.

d) *Content*

One clear conclusion emerges: the content of education for industrial democracy must be derived very closely from the learners' needs as they experience them. This raises the question of the definition of learning needs, and whether education for industrial democracy should be conceived of in terms of the transmission of knowledge or rather of the acquisition of skills, and how these skills are to be defined in relation to the perceived problems of the learners. The paradox is that for students to be able to articulate their own learning needs already presupposes a grasp of the context and relevance of the problems involved, and the achievement of this grasp is itself a process which presumably requires education.

In many cases, it is only towards the end of a particular session or course that the learner begins to be able to define and articulate his or her needs in relation to the issues dealt with (including the ability to dismiss them as irrelevant). There is, therefore, a constant process of learning being followed by, or at least accompanying, awareness of further learning needs, rather than being preceded by it. This presupposes an initial triggering factor, which may occur spontaneously or as a consequence of someone else's advice or suggestion.

There is thus a need to look at the most effective means of providing the initial trigger. One of the commonest pleas in overall adult education policy is for better information services and more generally for more effective ways of stimulating demand. The same is true for education for industrial democracy. Furthermore, how can subsequent learning needs be best built into courses so that the students' reaction to what they have just learnt is phrased not just as an evaluation of the past, but also as preferences for the future. These tend to presuppose a great degree of flexibility on the part of the providers. A third line of research under this heading, therefore, would be to look at the constraints which operate to limit such flexibility, whether they be organisational, attitudinal, financial, or other.

If we turn to the content itself, the suggestions which follow are tentative; they are provisional in the literal sense and they look forward in the expectation of being developed, modified, and discarded. For that reason, they will be only summarily treated.

First, there are *social* skills. We have already laid great stress on the collective aspects of industrial democracy and their educational consequences, and this can be linked directly to the actual acquisition of the skills needed to function in a group. Can such skills be acquired directly? Can existing disciplines contribute adequately to their development? For many people, "social skills" conjures up an image that mixes group therapy with questions of etiquette – can this be superseded?

Second, there are *communication* skills. These would also be relevant to social skills, but they are particularly important in any representative system of industrial democracy. There is the obvious need to be able to communicate to constituents the results of meetings and the reasons for decisions taken at them. But given the importance of construing communications as a two-way process, one could also include the capacity to elicit the views and feelings of other people. From the research point of view, this should not be limited to narrow technical considerations; there are much deeper issues of the modes of communication used and their symbolic content.

Third, there are the *technical* skills involved in the management of an enterprise. "Management" is to be understood in the broad sense, and indeed one of the more urgent research needs is a consideration of what the implications of industrial democracy are for the definition and development of managerial skills. For example, education for industrial democracy cannot be properly provided without including consideration of the way in which the production of goods or services is carried out.

Last, there is what can be broadly termed political education. This involves appreciation of the broad social and economic context of industrial democracy, and the way in which the behaviour of the individual enterprise is determined by that context. The fact that such a topic has an enormous scope prompts one final question as far as content is concerned: how can the myriad issues raised under this heading be covered within the time realistically available – however much provision could be expanded compared with what is currently available?

e) *The implications for the compilation and dissemination of knowledge*

We have so far argued that education for industrial democracy is concerned more with the acquisition of skills than the transmission of knowledge. If one expands the conception of knowledge to include the conceptual framework within which facts are accumulated and skills acquired, however, the growth of industrial democracy poses complex epistemological and political questions that deserve a prominent place on the research agenda.

First of all, it is worth mentioning the impact of new technology, especially electronic data processing and other developments in the field of information gathering and transmission. On the one hand, this must be analysed in terms of its impact on the nature of jobs, as to whether it accelerates the fragmentation of work and lowers the degree of job satisfaction. On the other hand, the potential of the technology for increasing the amount of information available and the speed with which it can be made available should not be ignored, especially in relation to the possibility of devolving decision-making. Here we have a powerful illustration of the potential links between occupational skills and education for industrial democracy.

Whatever the technology involved, however, one should look further than simply the information available, to investigate how it is used. What sorts of network – formal and informal – exist for the exchange of information, and how do the people situated at various points in those networks assimilate and use the knowledge that is at their disposal? Such questions are important both for understanding the decision-making process within an enterprise, and for assessing the calibre and power of bodies such as employer federations or shop-steward organisations which span several companies or several industries.

Behind this, however, is the whole question of the validation of knowledge. Linking the cliché that "knowledge is power" to the conception of industrial democracy as power sharing, one can plausibly argue that not only knowledge, but also control over what counts as knowledge, will have to be shared. Dominant interests maintain their dominance by defining what is and is not acceptable as truth or as professional expertise. A shift in the pattern of dominance, therefore, entails changes in the definitions offered and received. One approach to this issue is to scrutinise the current division of knowledge into its several disciplines. To expect participants to become competent in economics, politics, accountancy, and all the other fields relevant to enterprise decision-making is clearly absurd if the problems continue to be approached in terms of each discrete discipline. So, the basis for dividing knowledge into these particular fields may well be challenged.

Even within a given field, the criteria for validity may be called into question. The stock phrase used to describe accountancy practice is "true and fair", but it is obvious that these two terms have no absolute objective quality. Their application is determined largely by a traditional framework which ties them more or less firmly to the interests of capital. The emergence of the notion of a bilan social is an acknowledgement of the need to include in the analysis of a company's behaviour, items other than the mere return to capital. Is, for example, labour always to be regarded as a "cost", or should a company's balance sheet reveal what contribution it has made to providing stable and satisfying employment? How far should costs such as pollution effects be brought into the reckoning? Such questions reveal how a discipline may have to change within itself, even if it retains its discrete identity.

Which disciplines are involved? There are the traditional academic ones, some of which have been mentioned above: economics, politics, sociology and so on. Perhaps of more immediate relevance are some of the professionally oriented ones: in addition to accountancy, there is engineering, computer design, systems analysis, and education itself. Two other fields which merit special attention are management training and law.

More broadly, however, there is the critical problem of the criteria to be employed in defining knowledge. Just as we have suggested for methodology, the design and execution of research may themselves be included in the process of democratisation, so it can be argued that the fundamental notions of relevance and validity of knowledge are open to discussion. This should not be interpreted as a position of thoroughgoing relativism, with each participant encouraged to assert his or her views as true or valid without reference to any common corpus of accepted knowledge. The issue is, rather, how to arrive at a clearer understanding of the extent and nature of a common problem area.

BIBLIOGRAPHIC REFERENCES

1. E. Batstone (1984), *Working Order,* Blackwell, Oxford.
2. E. Batstone and L. P. Davies (1978), *Industrial Democracy: European Experience,* HMSO, London.
3. M. Carnoy and C.D. Shearer (1980), *Economic Democracy: The Challenge of the 1980s,* White Plains, New York.

4. C. Crouch and F. Heller (Eds.) (1983), *International Yearbook of Organizational Democracy*, Vol. I: *Organizational Democracy and Political Processes*, John Wiley, New York.
5. David Garson (1977), *Workers Self-Management in Industry: the West European Experience*, Praeger, New York.
6. Bjorn Gustavsen and Gerry Hunnins (1981), *New Patterns of Work Reform*, Universitetsforlaget, Oslo.
7. G. Hodgson (1984), *The Democratic Economy*, Penguin, London.
8. IDE (1982), Industrial Democracy in Europe, Oxford University Press.
9. Tom Schuller (1979), "The Democratization of Work: Educational Implications" in T. Schuller and J. Megarry (Eds.) *Recurrent Education and Lifelong Learning*, Kogan Page, London.
10. Tom Schuller (1985), *Democracy at Work*, Oxford University Press.
11. Robert Stern and Sharon McCarthy (Eds.) (1986), *International Yearbook of Organization Democracy*, Vol III: *The Organizational Practice of Democracy*, John Wiley, New York.

Part Two

THE ECONOMICS OF RECURRENT EDUCATION *

INTRODUCTION: THE ISSUES OF COST, BENEFITS AND FINANCING

The concept of recurrent education has been both enthusiastically advocated and bitterly attacked by economists in the last decade. While the basic idea that opportunities for education should be spread throughout life, not concentrated and confined to the early years, has been much debated in OECD countries and has influenced many recent educational developments and innovations, the original formula for recurrent education has nowhere been fully adopted. This may largely be due to its alleged economic implications, in particular prohibitive costs and questionable benefits. On the other hand, recurrent education is often advocated as a means of increasing the economic value of education by improving the links between education and work, making people more able to adjust to changing economic conditions, and overcoming obsolescence of skills due to technological change.

Thus, economic considerations are used both to support and to oppose the idea. For example, Blaug and Mace, attacking what they regard as the latest educational "bandwagon", and a "gigantic political balloon which collapses as soon as it is critically probed" argue that "if the recurrent education movement were to succeed, it would prove to be the most expansionary educational proposal that the world has ever seen. Fortunately, there is very little danger that it will succeed" (1). A much more sympathetic analysis of the economics of recurrent education by Stoikov concludes that recurrent education promises certain concrete benefits, but he also argues that cost-benefit analysis throws doubt on some of its aspects, in particular the notion that full-time higher education can usefully be postponed until later life (2). Such arguments emphasize that

---

* Grateful acknowledgement is made of the assistance rendered by a Group of Experts whose views on cost and financing of recurrent education have been taken into account in the presentation of this part of the report. This Group included: Professor Werner Clement of the School of Economics, Vienna; Dr. Andreas Fuchs, formerly Head of Division of the Joint Federal States Commission on Education Planning, Bonn, and presently Secretary of State, Ministry of Finance in the State of Bremen; Dr. Louis Emmerij, former Director of the Institute of Social Studies at the Hague and presently President of OECD's Development Centre; Professor Henry Levin, School of Education, Stanford University, Palo Alto, California; Professor Maurice Peston, Queen Mary College, University of London; Professor Gösta Rehn, former Director at OECD for Manpower, Education and Social Affairs and of the Institute for Social Research, Stockholm; Ms. Maureen Woodhall, Lecturer at the Institute of Education, University of London.

the opportunity costs of educating older workers are greater than the opportunity costs of higher education for young people immediately after secondary schooling, whereas the benefits will be lower, because of the shorter remaining working life. Other economists suggest that financial constraints reduce the viability of recurrent education, at a time when governments are reducing, rather than increasing, educational expenditure.

On the other hand, recent economic trends, in particular the increase in unemployment throughout OECD countries, mean that both the opportunity costs and the benefits of recurrent education must be reassessed. Peston, for example, argues that if the possibility of large-scale and persistent unemployment is taken into account, "the very nature of the question of recurrent education changes. .... Far from finance being a constraint on action which may also involve distortions due to resource misallocation, its costs are trivially small and, therefore, not constraining relative to its benefit. Instead of the question, 'Can we afford some education during working life?', we must ask, 'Can recurrent education be mounted on sufficiently large a scale and in an effective enough way to make full use of the human resources which are available for it and need it?'" (3). Similarly, Emmerij argues that to transform a "rigid sequential system" of education and training "into a more flexible recurrent system, in which it will be possible to combine or alternate periods of education, work and retirement throughout a person's adult life" would not impose a burden on public funds, and few, if any, additional funds would be required if social security funds were used creatively to finance recurrent education (4).

Thus, there appears to be a profound disagreement about the economic implications. Part of the dispute is concerned with the definition of recurrent education. The wider the definition, the more people would be included and the greater the cost. Stoikov, for example, discusses alternative definitions but adopts, for his discussion of the economics, a very wide one:

> A global system containing a variety of programmes which distribute education and training at different levels (primary, secondary and tertiary), by formal and non-formal means, over the life-span of the individual in a recurring way, that is alternated with work or other activities (5).

The costs of newly introducing such a "global system" would, indeed, be considerable, but it is often argued that many of the components of recurrent education already exist, but not in a sufficiently flexible and structured system. Emmerij, for example, argues that "recurrent education does not necessarily imply creating additional types of education and training, but the integration of existing types into one harmonious whole" (6).

An analysis of the economic implications therefore needs to consider at least four sets of questions:

> 1. To what extent would a system of recurrent education, which provides opportunities for education and training on a recurring basis, over a whole lifetime, by

means of alternating or combining education, work, leisure and retirement, differ from the present provision of post-secondary education?
2. What would be the costs of moving towards such a system, for the individual, for society as a whole, and for public funds?
3. What would be the economic, social, political or individual benefits of a system of recurrent education? Would such a system be more efficient and equitable than the present system, as its advocates have argued?
4. How could a system of recurrent education be financed? What changes would be needed in current financing mechanisms, and how would the costs of the system be shared between individuals, employers and the government?

The purpose of the following two chapters (Chapters V and VI) is to analyse the economic implications of recurrent education by looking at the first three groups of questions. Chapter VII considers various modes of and criteria for financing recurrent education, which has previously received relatively little attention in the literature.

NOTES AND REFERENCES

1. M. Blaug and J. Mace (1977), "Recurrent Education: The New Jerusalem", *Higher Education 6*, p. 277.
2. V. Stoikov (1975), *The Economics of Recurrent Education and Training*, Geneva: International Labour Office.
3. M. Peston (1979), "Recurrent Education: Tackling the Financial Implications", in Schuller/McGarry (1979), *Recurrent Education and Lifelong Learning*, World Yearbook of Education.
4. L. Emmerij (1983), "Paid Educational Leave: A Proposal Based on the Dutch Case", in H. Levin/H. G. Schütze (Eds.) (1983), *Financing Recurrent Education – Strategies for Increasing Employment, Job Opportunities and Productivity*, Beverly Hills (Sage) p. 297 ff., and in D. Kuhlenkamp/H. G. Schütze (Eds.), *Kosten und Finanzierung der beruflichen und nichtberuflichen Weiterbildung* (The Cost and Financing of Continuing Education and Training), Frankfurt (Diesterweg), 1982, p. 158.
5. V. Stoikov, op.cit., p. 5.
6. L. Emmerij, op.cit.

Chapter V
THE PRESENT PROVISION OF POST-COMPULSORY EDUCATION IN OECD COUNTRIES

1. *Scope of Survey*

Recurrent education, being a strategy for the distribution of education over the total life-span of the individual, envisages the incorporation of a number of provisions that are treated as distinct in most OECD countries. This means that any comparative consideration of the strategy's economic implications must take these provisions into account. The principal of them are:

- Post-compulsory secondary education;
- Post-secondary education, including all forms of higher education, both in universities and other institutions of higher education;
- Initial vocational training;
- Continuing vocational or professional training, including both on and off employers' premises;
- Retraining for unemployed workers;
- Adult education.

These various activities are separate entities in most countries, particularly as regards their financing. A system of recurrent education (if introduced) would, of course, have to treat them all as part of a comprehensive system, and what is more, would require proper co-ordination between them as to timing of courses, adjustment of admission rules and financial provisions for participants. We must say at once that it has proved impossible to come up with a fully comprehensive range of data on the provision, costs and financing of all of these varied activities. For example, figures are available on post-compulsory secondary education and on higher education, but for adult education and on-the-job training there are are not enough reliable data to be useful in the present context.

2. *Provision, Cost and Financing of Post-Compulsory Education*

The OECD attempted to estimate the level of participation and the costs of all forms of education for adults in a number of OECD countries but there were formidable problems in measuring the participation and costs of education for adults. The only relevant conclusion of this exercise was that if all forms of education and training are taken into account, then the extent of adult participation in education and training, and the total costs, "are considerable". Nevertheless, several of these studies pointed to the imbalance in the proportions of expenditure for adults and for young people. The Canadian study observed that "governments still cling to the myth that public responsibility for education is limited to that provided for children and youth with the result that a disproportionate share of national wealth is expended on education at the pre-adult level" (1).

A more recent review of strategies for financing recurrent education included a number of attempts in individual OECD countries to estimate the total participation and costs of all post-compulsory education (including regular upper secondary and higher education and also adult education and vocational teaching) (2). In the United States, for example, Wagner concluded that "in 1980, 50 million individuals participated in at least one type of organised post-secondary learning activity, at a total cost of $55 billion" (3). Tables 8 and 9 show that more than half of all enrolments are outside the regular post-secondary educational institutions, but more than 70 per cent of total expenditure on post-compulsory education and of total classroom hours is accounted for by educational institutions. The largest share of the total costs of instruction (43 per cent) was borne by higher educational institutions, but they accounted for only 20 per cent of total participation. Training by employers, including initial training through apprenticeships, off-the-job training in industry and training in the armed services accounted for 20 per cent of total costs, and 15 per cent of participation. These figures, however, only cover instruction and are far from representing the true opportunity cost, since the value of trainees' time is not included although, for employers, wages and salaries of trainees represent one of the major items of expenditure, and lost production one of the main opportunity costs of off-the-job training.

The picture that emerges from this survey in the United States is a considerable range of activities at the post-compulsory level, but with a preponderance of funding going to traditional, post-secondary institutions. The 1980 Education Amendments, enacted by Congress, had attempted to correct what was perceived as an imbalance in that adult learners were disproportionately young, white, well educated and earning salaries above the national median family income by financial and other measures to encourage aid available to more part-time students to help adults. However, in 1981, expenditure on student aid was reduced, as part of the overall cuts in the federal budget, and Christoffel had to conclude that "for the time being, the federal policy supporting recurrent education in this country, particularly that aimed at disadvantaged adults, is enacted in legislation but remains an opportunity deferred" (4).

The American pattern, both of provision and financing of post-compulsory education, therefore, continues to favour a period of uninterrupted education after compulsory schooling – the "front-end model" – which recurrent education is supposed to replace (5).

In the *United Kingdom*, the (now defunct) Advisory Council for Adult and Continuing Education (ACACE) carried out a survey of the entire field of educational opportunities for adults. The term "continuing education" is more widely used there than "recurrent education" but it similarly refers to a comprehensive strategy or system. ACACE explained that "by system we mean.... a

Table 8
UNITED STATES: PARTICIPATION IN POST–COMPULSORY EDUCTION AND TRAINING PROGRAMMES BY SOURCE, 1980

	Participants		Participant	Class Hours
	Number (thousands)	%	Number (millions)	%
TOTAL	74.850	100.0	8.950	100.0
POST–SECONDARY EDUCATIONAL INSTITUTIONS	31.350	41.9	6.350	71.0
Four-Year Colleges and Universities				
Full-Time	7.900	10.6	2.600	29.0
Part-Time	3.500	4.7	525	5.9
Non-Credit	3.100	4.2	75	.8
Two-Year Colleges				
Full-Time	2.000	2.7	650	7.3
Part-Time	2.700	3.6	350	3.9
Non-Credit	3.450	4.6	100	1.1
Vocational				
Full-Time	600	.8	450	5.0
Part-Time	3.000	4.0	550	6.1
Proprietary				
Full-Time	600	.8	450	5.0
Part-Time	3.000	4.0	550	6.1
Correspondence (civilian)	1.500	2.0	50	.6
OTHER POST–COMPULSORY EDUCATION AND TRAINING	43.500	58.1	2.600	29.0
Elementary and Secondary Schools	2.400	3.2	150	1.7
Business or Industry				
Apprentiicheships	700	.9	100	1.1
Other organized instruction (off-the-job)	7.400	9.9	400	4.5
Professional Associations	5.500	7.3	125	1.4
Labor Unions	100	.1	25	.3
Armed Forces				
Initial training	1.050	1.4	500	5.6
Other organized instruction	750	1.0	150	1.7
Correspondence	1.000	1.3	50	.6
Prisons	75	.1	25	.3
Other Government Programs				
Manpower training	975	1.3	325	3.6
Cooperative extension	5.100	6.8	75	.8
Other organized instruction (Off-the-job)	1.300	1.7	75	.8
Other Organized Programs (churches and synagouges, comunity organizations, libraries and museums, etc.	16.000	21.4	575	6.4
Tutors	1.150	1.5	25	.2

Source: A. Wagner, "An Inventory of Programs and Sources of Support in the U.S.", in H. Levin/H.G. Schütze (eds.) *Financing Recurrent Education* (1983).

Table 9
UNITED STATES: SELECTED MEASURES OF INSTRUCTIONAL COSTS OF POST–COMPULSORY EDUCTION AND TRAINING PROGRAMMES BY SOURCE, 1980

	Total Cost[a]		Per Program Participant[b] (in Dollars)	Per Participant Class HOur[c] (in Dollars)
	Dollars (millions)	%		
TOTAL	56.475	100.0	750	6.25
POST–SECONDARY EDUCATIONAL INSTITUTIONS	39.600	70.1	1.275	6.25
Four-Year Colleges and Universities	24.525	43.4	1.700	7.75
Two-Year Colleges	5.675	10.0	700	5.25
Vocational Schools	4.300	7.6	1.200	4.25
Proprietary Schools	4.050	7.2	1.125	4.00
OTHER POST–COMPULSARY EDUCATION AND TRAINING	16.874	29.9	400	6.50
Elementary and Secondary Schools	350	.6	150	2.75
Business or Industry Apprenticeships	350	.6	475	3.25
Other organised instruction (off-the-job)	7.200	12.7	975	18.00
Professional Associations	550	1.0	10	4.50
Labor Unions	25	*	225	7.25
Armed Forces				
Initial training	2.825	5.0		
Other organized instruction	775	5.00		
Correspondence	700	18.25		
Prisons	100	.2	1.225	4.50
Other Government Programs				
Manpower training	1.475	2.6	1.500	4.75
Cooperative Extension	350	.6	75	5.75
Other organized instruction (off-the-job)	575	1.0	450	6.50
Other Organized Programs (churches anbd synagogues, community organizations, libraries and museums, etc.)	1.500	2.6	100	2.75
Tutors	100	.2	100	4.00

Source: A. Wagner "An Inventory of Programs and Sources of Support in the U.S." in H. Levin/H.G. Schültze (Eds). *Financing Recurrent Education* (1983).

a. Rounded to nearest 25 million.
b. Rounded to nearest 25 dollars.
c. Rounded to nearest 25 cents.

* Less than .1%.

conjunction of policies, funding, provision and attitudes, which effect changes in all the present educational sectors to the advantage of a rapidly growing number of adult learners. In its essentials a system of continuing education is all that makes it increasingly possible for more and more adults to continue their education" (6). The report by ACACE on the future development of continuing education for adults advocates a "radical shift of emphasis by the whole post-school education system towards the educational needs of adults". The Council's survey of provisions for adults and costs covers post-secondary education, higher and further education in traditional institutions, enrolments in the Open University (which provides degree-level and post-experience courses for adults by distance teaching), adult education, industrial training by employers, and training or retraining in programmes organised by the Manpower Services Commission (MSC).

Although this adds up to a very considerable range of education opportunities for adults, the report shows that more than half the adult population of the United Kingdom have never engaged in any kind of education or training since completing their initial education.

The ACACE report permits a very rough estimate of the costs of continuing education by saying that about eight to nine per cent of GNP is devoted to all forms of education and training and that well over half of this goes to initial education. The proportion of educational public expenditure devoted to initial education is far higher: some 85 per cent. ACACE's final conclusion is to advocate a transformation of the existing pattern of education into a system of continuing education that it believes can be financed through the reallocation of existing resources without any significant additional funding.

There have been some more recent developments in the United Kingdom, designed to strengthen continuing vocational education for adults. The Manpower Services Commission is spending some ö250 million annually on adult training programmes, including special programmes for long-term unemployed adults, and for women who want to undertake training or retraining after interrupting their careers, when, in 1982, a new initiative was launched to provide mid-career vocational education for workers wishing to update their skills. This is known as PICKUP (Professional, Industrial and Commercial Updating). Other recent initiatives include "Open College" and "Open Tech" programmes. A Government White Paper on *Training for Jobs,* published in 1984, proposed expanding and restructuring adult training programmes to provide opportunities for 250 000, including 125 000 unemployed adults. Another significant development in 1984 was the publication of a report on continuing education which drew attention to the increasing importance of post-experience vocational education in universities, a development which is likely to continue and increase (7).

In the United Kingdom in 1980-81, mature students (25 or over), constituted about 25 per cent of all students in universities, polytechnics and colleges of further education. The proportion of over 25s entering universities alone for first degree courses, however, was only about five per cent. Put another way: mature students are more likely to study at a non-university institution and the majority of them do so as part-timers, rather than full-timers. More than half of all students entering higher education of any kind and on whatever basis are aged 20 or younger, and only 28 per cent of new entrants to higher education are over the age of 24 (8).

The situation is different in *Sweden,* where over 63 per cent of all students in higher education are over 24. The Higher Education Act, which was enacted in 1977, established recurrent education as a basic principle in planning higher education. The subsequent reform of higher education aimed to expand the opportunities for adults to alternate periods of study with employment or family care. Admission criteria were changed to allow students to qualify for admission to higher education through work experience as well as academic qualifications, through the "25/4 rule" which let in over 25s who had at least four years of work experience. Teaching methods have been changed to cater for adult students; for example, evening classes are provided and distance teaching has been introduced in all the higher education institutions. New short-cycle courses of vocational-technical education and training have been developed for students who have worked for a number of years in the appropriate industry.

In addition to these opportunities, there is a very wide range of adult education provisions which include study circles, residential adult colleges, folk high schools and a new development, "outreach programmes", for people with less than nine years of schooling and are run by trade unions and voluntary education associations (9). Finally, the National Labour Market Board provides labour market training for those who are unemployed or in danger of it.

Both higher education and adult education are heavily subsidised in Sweden, and the system of aid for students provides a mixture of loans and grants for those in higher education ("Study Means") and study allowances to compensate for loss of income for adults taking short courses, attending folk high schools or study circles ("Study Benefit") (10). All Swedish workers have the right to study leave, with a guaranteed right to return to their job after completing their course. The right to paid education leave (PEL) is examined below, but it should be noted here that in Sweden educational leave of absence is unpaid. However, the student aid system provides hourly or daily student grants for workers who take time off work to attend courses, and allowances for those pursuing longer, uninterrupted courses of study, but the regulations state:

> Resources are limited, and not all those formally entitled to this benefit will be able to receive it in reality. Priority is therefore given to those with the greatest need of education and assistance. ... Competition is stiff and experience shows that the only applicants who are normally granted such assistance are those who:

- Have only a basic seven-year or nine-year schooling behind them;
- Have been gainfully employed for at least ten years;
- Are at least 30 years old (11).

In fact, more than half of all students in higher education are 25 years and older and it is estimated that at least a third of Sweden's adult population pursues studies in one form or another, which means that the concept of recurrent education finds greater expression in Sweden than elsewhere in the OECD area. Nevertheless, surveys still show that the chief beneficiaries are those who already have educational qualifications, and a recent report for OECD emphasizes that the fact that students over 25 are in the majority in Swedish higher education does not imply strong participation of so-called underprivileged adults with a restricted educational background: "Thus, the Swedish system is not as open as one tends to believe" (12).

In *Germany* it has been stipulated, and in fact declared to be a principle of educational policy, that continuing education (*Weiterbildung*) should be developed to become a veritable fourth sector of education, on equal footing with the primary, secondary and higher sectors. This is defined as "the continuation or resumption of all kinds of organised learning upon completion of an initial education which can be of varying lengths and which commonly comes to an end with entering working life". We have here, therefore, something very different from the concept of recurrent education that would provide access to the whole gamut of post-compulsory education and training.

Higher education in the Federal Republic is seen as part of initial education and a number of aspects of the German system makes it next to impossible to pursue higher education in a recurrent fashion. For example, attendance for students aiming at a higher-education degree is full-time (with the exception only of enrolment in the Distance University at Hagen where students can choose to study half-time); and studies must be pursued once they have been embarked upon, without interruption, and exceptions to this are granted only in very limited cases, such as sickness or comparable emergency situations. Furthermore, the law governing student aid contains an age ceiling which excludes new entrants above the age of 30 – except in narrowly regulated cases. Such an age ceiling is also attached to the family allowance scheme under which studying children without an income of their own entitle their parents to draw family allowance up to the completion of 27 years.

As a consequence of these restricting factors, participation of adults in university-type higher-education degree courses in Germany is comparatively low: less than ten per cent of new entrants are 25 years and over (see Table 10a). These figures include the 13 000 adult degree students (80 per cent of whom study half-time) enrolled in the Distance University.

Table 10a
PERCENTAGE DISTRIBUTION BY AGE OF NEW ENTRANTS IN THE THIRD–LEVEL EDUCATION; UNIVERSITY–TYPE HIGHER EDUCATION (1) (1981)*

Country	Male	Female	Country	Male	Female
Australia			*Italy*		
Under 20	46.7	51.1	Under 20	46.3	66.1
20–24	20.0	16.5	20–24	38.3	26.5
25 and over	32.7	32.3	25 and over	15.0	7.4
Austria			*Netherlands*		
Under 20	59.6	73.2	Under 20	57.3	52.6
20–24	34.4	20.2	20–24	29.7	23.5
25 and over	6.0	6.8	25 and over	13.0	13.9
Denmark			*New Zealand*		
Under 20	11.0	10.0	Under 20	70.2	68.5
20–24	56.0	60.8	20–24	17.6	15.4
25 and over	33.0	29.2	25 and over	12.2	16.1
Finland			*Spain*		
Under 20	31.3	33.3	Under 20	69.1	70.5
20–24	55.2	53.1	20–24	14.0	13.0
25 and over	13.4	13.6	25 and over	16.9	16.5
France			*Sweden*		
Under 20	57.9	69.6	Over 25	46.8	52.7
20–23	28.0	20.3	Of which admitted according to 25/4 scheme (2)	22.7	25.3
24 and over	14.1	10.1			
Germany			*United Kingdom*		
Under 20	13.9	37.7	Under 20	62.6	57.4
20–24	74.7	54.7	20	4.6	4.8
25 and over	11.4	7.5	21–24	18.4	19.7
			25 and over	14.4	18.1
Greece					
Under 20	61.3	80.7			
20–24	38.7	26.5			
25 and over	15.0	7.4			

Source: OECD Education Data Bank (National Statistical Yearbooks — verified by countries)

Tables 10a and 10b are from OECD/CERI, *Participation of Adults in Higher Education*, Paris 1986.

*Or nearest year

Notes:
1. *Australia* — data refer to universities, colleges of advanced education and non-government (private) tertiary colleges.
   Finland — data refer to universities and degree-granting institutions.
   Germany — universities and degree-granting institutions.
   New Zealand — universities and teacher training colleges.
   United Kingdom — full-time only; includes 31 000 post-graduate students, excludes 65 268 open university students aged 25 or over.

2. The 25/4 scheme is a special admission scheme requiring 25 years of age and five years of work experience instead of traditional academic entry requirements.

Table 10b
PERCENTAGE DISTRIBUTION BY AGE OF NEW ENTRANTS IN THIRD-LEVEL EDUCATION; NON-UNIVERSITY HIGHER EDUCATION (1981)*

Country	Male	Female	Country	Male	Female
AUSTRALIA			GREECE		
Full-Time			Under 20	57.4	76.4
			20-24	37.2	27.3
Under 20	76.7	82.5	25 and over	5.4	1.3
20-24	13.7	7.5			
25 and over	11.1	10.0	SWEDEN (1)		
Part-Time			Under 20	7.9	10.7
			20-24	41.7	30.8
Under 20	28.3	26.1	25 and over	50.4	57.9
20-24	24.7	20.5			
25 and over	47.1	53.3	UNITED KINGDOM		
			20 and under	43.3	46.4
FRANCE			21-24	25.2	20.7
			25 and over	31.5	32.9
Under 20	69.3	83.3			
20-24	28.9	15.6			
25 and over	1.8	1.1			
GERMANY					
Under 20	9.9	30.2			
20-24	76.8	60.3			
25 and over	13.3	9.3			

Source: OECD Education Data Bank (National Statistical Yearbooks — verified by countries).

* or nearest year.

1. Students in undergraduate education in higher education institutions.

Table 11
GERMANY: PUBLIC EXPENDITURE (FEDERAL, LÄNDER AND LOCAL AUTHORITIES) FOR SCHOOLS, INSTITUTIONS OF HIGHER EDUCATION AND FOR CONTINUING EDUCATION AND TRAINING, 1970-1985
(in billion Deutschmarks (DM) and as percentage of GNP (%))

			1970	1975	1980	1985
I. Initial Education and Training	Schools and Higher Education	DM	24.00	46.4	61.60	68.20
		%	3.55	4.51	4.14	3.72
	Student Aid	DM	–	2.60	3.60	2.30
		%	–	0.25	0.24	0.13
	Total	DM	23.50	49.20	64.90	70.50
		%	3.45	4.76	4.36	3.85
II. Continuing Education and Training	Continuing Education and Training	DM	0.60	1.1	2.30	2.60
		%	0.09	0.1	0.15	0.14
	Labour Market Training (1)	DM	0.9	3.3	4.6	5.90
		%	0.13	0.32	0.31	0.32
	Total	DM	1.50	4.40	6.70	8.5
		%	0.21	0.43	0.45	0.46

1. Continuing training, retraining, on-the-job training, under the auspices of the Federal Labour Administration.

Source: Federal Ministry for Education and Science, Basic and Structural Data, Bonn, 1986/87.

Table 12
GERMANY: PUBLIC AND PRIVATE EXPENDITURE FOR INITIAL AND CONTINUING EDUCATION AND TRAINING, 1970-1984
[in billion Deutschmarks (DM) and as percentage of GNP (%)]

		1970	1975	1980	1984
A. *PUBLIC EXPENDITURE*					
I. Initial Education and Training (including higher education) and Student Aid	DM	24.0	49.0	65.2	69.5
	%	3.55	4.76	4.34	3.96
II. Continuing Education and Training (including labour market training)	DM	1.50	4.40	6.90	8.20
	%	0.21	0.43	0.46	0.47

B. *PRIVATE SECTOR EXPENDITURE*

III. Overall Vocational Training	DM	6.90	10.00	15.50	30.8
	%	1.02	0.97	1.04	1.76
of which: Continuing Training and Retraining	DM	n.a.	n.a.	n.a.	9.6
	%	–	–	–	0.55

Source: Federal Ministry for Education and Science, Basic and Structural Data, Bonn, 1985/86.

With the exception of higher education finance, which is relatively simple in operation, continuing education finance is characterised by a great variety of sources and of modes of financing. Due to this variety, consistent data about participation and costs are hard to come by but there are a number of recent studies which shed light on the continuing education sector (13). Regarding the cost involved, the relative increase of public outlays here during 1982 was bigger than for schools and higher education, although these too expanded fast until the mid-1970s when they started to level off. However, in spite of this disproportionate growth rate, continuing education has a relatively small share of both the overall educational budget and the gross national budget (Table 11). Thus continuing education is not only the poor relative of the formal school system in general but also of the higher education system (the public outlays in 1985 for higher education were DM 21.4 billion – or 23.7 billion counting student aid – as compared to DM 8.5 billion spent on continuing education, including labour market training).

These figures do not, of course, include outlays of the private sector or individuals who finance their own expenses for continuing education. As in other countries, estimates for business and industry vary widely. It has been estimated, however, that the total expenditure for vocational training incurred by the private sector has risen from around DM 7 billion in 1970 to approximately DM 31 billion in 1984. Of this latter amount, around one-third is spent for continuing training and retraining of the workforce (cf. Table 12); but this estimate does not take into account the fact that outlays for training are set off against the tax bill and thus a considerable share is indirectly financed by the taxpayer. It must also be noted when comparing public and private expenditure that public expenditure figures do not include wages or salaries of students and trainees while private sector calculations do. An exception are the figures for continuing training and retraining under the auspices of the Federal Labour Administration, where the outlays for instruction and instruction-related costs represent approximately one-third only of the total expenses incurred, while the remainder pays for income maintenance (14).

In *France*, payroll taxes help to finance continuing vocational training through a system of training funds, which also receive public funding. The 1971 Act on Continuing Professional Training (*Loi portant sur l'organisation de la formation professionnelle continue dans le cadre de l'éducation permanente*) made it mandatory for firms employing more than ten persons to devote at least 0.8 per cent of their wage bill to spending for continuing training of the workforce. The current mandatory contribution is 1.1 per cent for training activities inside or outside the enterprise. Any of this unspent must be paid into the French Treasury (15).

In 1982, 3.2 million workers and employees in the private sector (one out of six) participated in some organised training activity averaging 120 hours per employee. The budget for continuing training under the 1971 Act amounted to some FF. 26 billion in 1982, of which the enterprises bore almost 15 billion while the remaining 11 billion were assumed by the State. In 1984, the Act was amended mainly to increase the chances of employees taking paid educational leave to pursue courses of their own choice outside the enterprise. The amendment has not, however, changed the 1.1 per cent wage bill rate so that the total outlays for training are not expected to change dramatically.

While most training in France takes place in the enterprise, there are a good many outside training institutions that provide courses, particularly for highly qualified personnel. In 1981, for instance, some 170 000 employees participated in programmes offered by universities, the fees being paid by their employers.

The growing role of university-provided courses which are vocationally oriented does not imply, however, a general policy of open access of adults to institutions of higher education. Degree-seeking adults must hold adequate entrance qualifications, with the exception of a number of degree programmes in engineering administered by the Conservatoire National des Arts et Måtiers where previous technical training and related work experience are sufficient for admission. A special university entrance exam has to be passed by adults who do not hold a baccalauréat or its equivalent and not all universities offer courses in preparation for this. Although the number of candidates is steadily growing, it is still unimpressive compared to overall student enrolment.

3. *Paid Educational Leave*

No review of the concept of lifelong learning in recurrent education would be complete without a look at developments in *Paid Educational Leave* (PEL) that have been taking place over the last decade.

The realisation of recurrent education as a strategy for lifelong learning has always envisaged something like PEL as an essential mechanism for enabling adults to alternate between work and educational activities (16). The 1974 Convention and Recommendations on Paid Educational Leave adopted by the International Labour Office (ILO) defines it as "leave granted to a worker for educational purposes for a specified period during working hours, with adequate financial entitlements", and countries adopting the Convention commit themselves "to formulate and apply a policy designed to promote, by methods appropriate to national conditions and practice and by stages as necessary, the granting of paid educational leave for the purpose of training at any level, generally, social and civic education (as well as) trade-union education".

While most OECD Member countries have ratified the ILO Convention, there are important country-specific differences as to the definition, policies and practices of educational leave. For example, while continuing education and training provided by enterprises for employees, is considered as educational leave in Great Britain, this does not qualify as "leave" in the Federal Republic of Germany or in France. Another divergence occurs with respect to "adequate financial entitlements". In several European countries provision for educational leave is automatically linked to financial support, while in other countries it is not, and financial support is provided only for specific groups or for certain kinds of educational activities.

Educational leave schemes exist in a wide variety of forms and, in some countries there are systems of alternating between work and education that do not fall within the ILO definition. For example, in Germany, Austria and Switzerland, who have a so-called "dual system" of initial vocational training, an employer who provides apprenticeship training is obliged by law to release apprentices for vocational school attendance, either one to two days per week or in the form of block release. Although this scheme seems to represent a perfect example of educational leave, it does not properly qualify as such, since in these countries young people are legally obliged to attend vocational school on a part-time basis, usually up to the age of 18. This period of training is therefore part of the compulsory education of young people, and school attendance under this scheme is not an individual right but a duty.

Most Western European countries also provide full-time or part-time training schemes for the unemployed whose objective is to help the participants get back into employment, but this also should not be regarded as PEL. Educational leave, in the sense of an employee's right to take leave for educational purposes, is commonly understood as having two principal components: first, time off work for learning and, second, job security. Since the element of job security – in the sense of a guarantee to return to the job previously held – is lacking, for the unemployed, or for participants of labour market training programmes who retrain for completely different jobs, such training or retraining programmes should not properly be defined as PEL.

At present there are only four Western European countries with general educational leave legislation that is not limited to specific occupations or categories of employees. A notable example of such legislation is the French Law of 1971, the objective of which is to enable workers to adapt to changes in the techniques and conditions of work, to encourage their social mobility and their own contributions to cultural, economic and social development.

In the past, PEL, in the sense of leave taken on the employee's rather than the employer's initiative, has played a minor role in comparison with employer-provided or employer-sponsored training in France. The main reason is that the right to leave was not directly connected to the right to remuneration, which was governed by a complicated and often confusing set of regulations, depending on the accreditation of the training programme, its duration and the occupational status of the trainee. It was largely due to such confusion that the number of participants was low and the trend of participation has declined.

We have already said, in effect, that one of the objectives of the 1984 amendment to the 1971 Law was to facilitate PEL. It gives a right to paid educational leave to any employee who has worked for at least six months or who has two years of seniority, of which six months must have been spent in his present firm. The maximum duration of the programme is one year, or 1 200 hours part-time, and leave may be taken for professional or broader cultural courses. The employer is obliged to maintain a certain percentage of the remuneration that the employee would have received had he stayed on the job, but he is in turn reimbursed by a collective fund to which he is required to contribute 0.1 per cent of his wages. It is too early to see the results of this new measure, but the setting aside of almost ten per cent of the total amount required by the law to be spent on continuing training will undoubtedly do much to enhance participation in PEL.

Another country with a legally established system of educational leave is *Belgium* which in 1973 established the "Law on Credit Hours". Eligibility and the amount of leave entitlement under this law are dependent on previous participation in accredited continuing education and training courses. In other words, workers' credit is accorded to self-initiated participation in a recognised education or training course undertaken outside working hours. Approved courses were initially limited to vocational training, the provision has been enlarged to include courses in music, litterature, the arts and general education including university courses. Only employees under 40 are eligible.

The scheme is somewhat larger than it might seem, for even a student enrolled in a first year course can obtain compensation in credit hours equal to 25 per cent of the course he is taking, and an employee who has participated in a course outside working hours for a total of two hours is eligible for the necessary time off to complete his course.

The most important factor affecting the utilisation of the entitlement is, of course, a guarantee that time off work is compensated by a concomitant right to remuneration. In Belgium the right to leave automatically connotes the right to a financial recompense during time off work; but this remuneration is provided at the level of the legal minimum wage and thus entails a significant sacrifice in terms of earnings for most employees.

The financing of the credit-hour scheme is administered by a central fund, financed by a compulsory wage bill levy. Initially, in 1973, this levy amounted to 0.3 per cent of the payroll, but has since been reduced to its present level of

0.03 per cent — a vivid illustration of how the scheme is being underused and the low level of financial assistance provided to employees, who suffer considerable loss of income during educational leave.

In summary, it is probably fair to say that because of its design, the present Belgian scheme of credit hours has been marginal in importance. However, discussions regarding its reform are under way and both employers and trade unions agree that the age ceiling must be eliminated and that the present concept of "credit hours" (i.e. a system of compensation for leisure time sacrificed for education and training) ought to be replaced by a system of general eligibility for participation in educational and training activities during working time which would not be dependent on previous participation in training. Of course, the employers favour courses with an emphasis on vocational training; while they are ready to bear 50 per cent of the costs of such courses, they argue that general and civic education should be financed by the State.

As in the United States or Canada, the states in Germany, the Länder, have the power to regulate educational matters autonomously, while the Federal Government has very limited jurisdiction in this area. However, since the Constitution vests the power to legislate on economic and labour market matters in the Federal Government, it is authorised to pass legislation on educational leave. Since, however, the Federal Government has backed away from earlier plans to introduce such legislation, educational leave laws have been passed by six of the Länder, including West Berlin (17).

These Länder laws have differing features as to eligibility and accreditation. For example in four, accreditable courses are limited to continuing vocational training and civic education, but in the state of Bremen continuing general education is included in the range. The basic provision, however, is identical in almost all in that the laws give beneficiaries the right to leave for one working week per year (Berlin: two working weeks) or cumulatively for two working weeks (8 working days in Lower Saxony) for two consecutive years, during which period a worker's salary or wage is maintained in full by the employer. In Berlin, there is an age ceiling limiting eligibility to apprentices and young workers or employees up to age 25. This, of course, is a major restriction eliminating the majority of the working population.

While the objective of *continuing vocational training* is to better qualifications and occupational flexibility, there is no clearly spelled out definition of *general education* in the laws of the two states that include it in their approved courses. This has led to difficulties when employers have refused to grant leave for general courses such as full-time language programmes not related to job requirements. Some workers have carried their cause to the labour courts which have, in the first instance, ruled that such courses are indeed covered by the term of "general education". While results of these cases are pending before the Supreme Labour Court, there is growing resistance among employers against paid leave for what are seen as leisure time activities. It is likely that this resistance will lead to a revision of the law.

Participation in PEL under the existing Länder laws is in general low (between 2 and 6 per cent of eligible workers and employees). The schemes have thus neither lived up to the aspirations of the trade unions who were the driving force behind the legislation, nor warranted the fears of the employers who resisted it mainly on the grounds of cost. In two of the states (Hesse and Northrhine Westfalia) the State Employers' Associations have challenged the constitutional basis of PEL laws (decisions still pending, December 1986).

In summary, the German experience suggests that PEL is being widely underutilised, for a variety of reasons but mainly because of opposition from employers and concern by workers about leaving their jobs when unemployment levels are high. Nevertheless, as a result of state legislation, a large group of workers and employees do undertake some kind of further education and training each year. Most of this group have traditionally been under-represented in continuing education and training and it is fair to say that they probably would not have participated without educational leave.

Although *Sweden* has a long-standing tradition of adult education, it was not until 1st January 1975 that a generally applicable law on educational leave came into effect. This law secures the right of all employees, in both the public and private sector, to take leave for educational purposes during working hours.

It is remarkable for a number of reasons. First, the right to educational leave covers all types of education and vocational training, as well as trade-union education. Second, the duration of the leave is dependent on the length of the course chosen; no maximum is set. But, while the law is so generous as to the range of eligible activities and the duration of leave, it is silent about the financial arrangements. In other words, it provides for educational leave but not for *paid* educational leave, deflecting the question of financial support to other laws.

Financial assistance for those taking advantage of their right to educational leave is available under three different schemes: "AMS" grants, Study Assistance and Adult Study Assistance. The first provides for financial assistance to trainees undergoing labour market training (unemployed persons or those who are threatened by unemployment) and thus, in most cases, does not apply to genuine educational leave of absence as defined above. *Study assistance* is a mixed system of grants and loans for upper secondary and post-secondary students. There are age restrictions: for example, upper secondary students must be twenty or older, and students over 50 are normally excluded. The loan portion of the scheme is considerable: between 80 and 90 per cent of the student support (which amounts to about two-thirds of average industrial earnings after tax) is repayable. In addition to a means test, support under this scheme is also dependent on academic achievement. Loans must be repaid in instalments, starting two years after completion of studies, and while there is no regular interest to be paid on the debt, loans are adjusted annually according to an adjustment index (18).

The *Adult Study Assistance Scheme,* introduced in 1976, consists of several sub-schemes targeted at undereducated adults who wish to pursue full-time or part-time education in order to obtain formal educational qualifications. The Scheme is financed by a payroll tax, at present 0.25 per cent, yielding a total of around S.Kr. 590 million in 1980-81. The sub-schemes reflect three basic forms of financial assistance for adults. First, assistance for prolonged periods of (primarily) academic study at elementary and secondary school level. At the post-secondary level, it is only available to those enrolled in vocational education. The main eligibility criterion is four years of previous employment, or comparable social activities (e.g. child rearing), and there is a (normal) age ceiling of 45. In 1980-81, a total of 15 800 full-time grants were made under this programme. Secondly, under the Adult Assistance Scheme there is an hourly study assistance payable to people who participate in study circles and incur loss of earnings as a result. This is available only for certain kinds of course – those covering topics in the elementary school curriculum, education courses for trade-union members, and special courses for handicapped persons. Thirdly, there is a daily study assistance which makes it possible to combine study circle attendance with short-term courses (19).

While general educational leave legislation is limited to a few countries, most have some legal provision for specific populations, groups or employees with particular functions or responsibilities (20). Most important, in terms of numbers affected, is probably the right of trade-union officials or elected members of enterprise councils to time off during working hours for courses preparing them for their union responsibilities. Such a legal right exists in Germany (where the leave is paid), France and Sweden (where it is unpaid). It is also often contained in collective bargaining agreements. Comparable rights exist in some countries for health and security officers in enterprises, representatives of handicapped employees (Germany), or immigrants who are eligible for up to 240 hours of paid leave in order to learn the country's language (Sweden). Many countries have leave provisions for employees in public service, most often for teachers, but also for judges or others. Nevertheless, even for these groups, participation in continuing education during work time is very often a privilege, rather than a right, in the sense that it could be successfully claimed or enforced in court if an employer refused to grant it.

Several West European countries have left PEL to the employers and unions, as a matter for collective bargaining. Most prominent among these is *Italy* whose "150 hours" scheme is widely known.

Although there is no legislation for general PEL in Italy, there is a law (1970) that stipulates the right of workers to time off during working hours to enroll in recognised courses in primary, secondary and technical schools, and sit for examinations. Nothing, however, is said about remuneration so this question is left to the bargaining process. A collective agreement between employers and the metal workers' union, struck in 1973, has become a model for basically similar agreements adopted by other sectors of industry. There are two distinguishing features about this agreement.

First, the right to leave is conceived as a collective rather than an individual right, because time off during working hours is granted to the workers of a firm as a group. Paid leave for study purposes is allotted in a block to the total personnel in the form of a fund of available leave hours, the amount of which is calculated as a function of the number of workers employed in the firm. The individual worker can use a maximum of 150 hours over a three-year period – hence, the name of the scheme. The leave is granted on the condition that workers devote as many leisure hours to study as the number of hours of PEL provided from the collective fund. The decision as to which individual workers will profit from the collectivity fund, (i.e. the distribution of available leave time) lies with the enterprise council rather than the employer.

The second interesting feature of the scheme is that the primary beneficiaries are workers who are short on previous educational attainment, and who use the scheme to pass the *licencia media,* i.e. the lower secondary school diploma. This *licencia* is of particular importance, since it is a prerequisite for both job opportunities in the public sector and for participation in most vocational training programmes. One of the major problems in using the 150 hours scheme for this purpose is that the courses require 350 to 400 hours' attendance; so participants must provide 250 hours or so of their own private time even before allowing for individual study and preparation. Nevertheless, participation in these courses has been significant, amounting to around 90 to 100 thousand adults each year (21).

In the other European countries where leave schemes can be found in collective bargaining agreements, the impact has been relatively minor. In the United Kingdom, the situation varies considerably since the granting of educational leave lies at the discretion of employers; it is not an individual right of the employee. There is no obligation on employers to maintain a worker's wages during attendance, or to pay for the costs of the course, and when paid educational leave is granted it is generally for the purpose of vocational training, and it is the employer who selects employees for participation in training courses. In a nutshell, it is fair to say that PEL is not yet an established part of training policies, although a study of PEL in England and Wales estimated that over three million people received some form of PEL in 1976/77 (22).

Finally, Germany must again be mentioned since some 200 collective bargaining agreements establish the right to educational leave, though not all of them entail payment and the majority are limited to enterprise council members. Eligibility under these schemes overlap to a considerable extent with the legal provisions for paid educational leave which we have already discussed. The two types of rights are not mutually exclusive in principle, although in actual practice they mostly are (23).

What then are we to conclude about the acceptance/adoption of the concept of educational leave in Western Europe?

First that, while there has been no universal, sweeping movement in its favour, many countries have achieved some kind of provision for educational leave – albeit there being much variation between them. The map, however, still reveals some important blank spots, (notably Denmark, Austria, Switzerland, the Netherlands, Spain, Portugal, Greece). The Netherlands (24) are feeling their way towards it.

Next we must take note of a slow development and low participation rates in existing schemes. The reasons for this are various: general economic conditions, unemployment, lack of sufficient financial support, inadequacy of suitable courses and of outreach programmes for the underprivileged. On the other hand, it is undeniable that demand is increasing and that lifelong learning in a recurrent pattern is now more widely accepted both as an individual right and as a necessary response to rapid technological and social change.

Assessment of the actual impact of educational leave in Europe is extremely difficult. As an instrument influencing the supply side of the labour market it has had only a marginal effect, or none at all. There are many examples of low overall participation and of short average leave duration; the provisions contained in most laws or agreements are designed to avoid a situation whereby too many workers of the same firm use their leave entitlement simultaneously, thus obliging the enterprise to hire additional staff (25). Other possible effects (though impossible to quantify) may be on the social climate in the enterprise, individual flexibility and employability, and productivity as a result of a higher standard of both vocational and general education (26).

So, although there is growing evidence in OECD countries of the influence of the concept of recurrent education, and although there has been an increase in availability of educational opportunities for adults, these opportunities are still fragmented, and the emphasis in most countries, both in provision and financing, is on the "front-end model" with the bulk of post-compulsory education and initial training taking place immediately after compulsory schooling. Do economic considerations make this inevitable? What would be the economic costs and benefits of accelerating the movement towards a recurrent model? The following chapter concentrates on this question.

NOTES AND REFERENCES

1. OECD (1977), *Learning Opportunities for Adults: Volume IV, Participation in Adult Education*, Paris, OECD, p. 109.
2. H. Levin and H. G. Schütze (Eds.) (1983), *Strategies for Increasing Employment, Job Opportunities and Productivity*, Beverly Hills (Sage).

3. A. P. Wagner (1983), "Financing Recurrent Education in the United States: An Inventory of Programs and Sources of Support", in Levin/Schütze, *op. cit.*, pp. 133-158.
4. P.H. Christoffel (1983), "An Opportunity Deferred: Lifelong Learning in the United States", in Levin/Schütze, *op.cit.*, pp. 225-234.
5. H. Levin and H. G. Schütze (1983), "Economic and Political Dimensions of Recurrent Education", in Levin/Schütze, *op.cit.*, pp. 9-36.
6. Advisory Council for Adult and Continuing Education (ACACE) (1982): *Continuing Education: From Policies to Practice.* Leicester (ACACE, p. vii.
7. University Grants Committee (UGC), *Report of Continuing Education Working Party* (chaired by R.S. Johnson), London: UGC 1984.
8. Cf. M. Slowey (1987), "Participation of Adults in Higher Education: Survey of the Situation in England and Wales", in H. G. Schütze (Ed.), *The Participation of Adults in Higher Education in the U.K., the U S. and Canada,* Stockholm (Almqvist & Wiksell International).
9. For a description of outreach programmes in Sweden, see OECD (1976) *Developments in Educational Leave of Absence,* Paris, OECD, p. 191-4.
10. For an account of the Swedish system of student financial aid see M. Woodhall (1982), *Student Loans: Lessons from Recent International Experience.* London, Policy Studies Institute.
11. Centrala Studiestöds Nämnden (CSN) (1981), *A Survey of National Benefits for Students.* Sundsvall, CSN.
12. K. Abrahamsson (1986), *The Participation of Adults in Swedish Higher Education,* Stockholm (Almqvist & Wiksell); see also K. Rubenson (1983) "Educational Leave in Sweden," in H. Levin/ H. G. Schütze, *op. cit.*
13. Cf. F. Edding (1983) "Die Finanzierung der Weiterbildung – Fakten und Probleme" (Financing Continuing Education in the Federal Republic – Facts and Problems), in D. Kuhlenkamp/H.G. Schtze (Eds.), *Kosten und Finanzierung der beruflichen und nichtberuflichen Weiterbildung* (The Cost and Financing of Continuing Education and Training), Frankfurt (Diesterweg) 1982.
14. Cf. H. G. Schütze (1983), "Financing Paid Educational Leave in the Federal Republic of Germany", in H. Levin/H.G. Schütze, *op. cit.*
15. For details cf. P. Caspar (1983), "French Law on Continuing Vocational Training", in: Levin/Schütze, *op. cit.*, pp. 257-272.
16. OECD/CERI (1973) *Recurrent Education: A Strategy for Lifelong Learning,* Paris, p. 28.
17. For further details see H.G. Schütze (1983), op.cit., in H. Levin/ H.G. Schütze (Eds.), *op.cit.*, pp. 273-296.
18. For details see K. Rubenson, "Educational Leave in Sweden", in H. Levin/H.G. Schütze (Eds.), *op.cit.*, pp. 237-255.
19. This rather complex system of student support makes it very difficult to assess the financial assistance schemes in their effect on utilisation of edu-

cational leave. But see the detailed discussion by K. Rubenson, *op.cit.*
20. Cf. the overview on special leave in ten countries in the *European Industrial Relations Review*, May 1982, pp. 12-17.
21. S. Bruno, "Educational Leave in Italy", in D. Kuhlenkamp/H.G. Schütze (Eds.), *op. cit.*
22. J. Killeen and M. Bird, *Education and Work: A Study of Paid Educational Leave in England*, and I. O'Malley, "Paid Educational Leave in Australia, Canada, Ireland and the United Kingdom", in *International Labour Review*, Vol. 121 (1982) pp.169-183.
23. Cf. H.G. Schütze, opË citË, in Levin/Schütze, *op.cit.*
24. See for example L. Emmerij, "Paid Educational Leave: A Proposal Based on the Dutch Case", in Levin and Schütze, op.cit.
25. D. Degen and E. Nuissl, *Educational Leave and the Labour Market in Europe*, Berlin (European Center for Vocational Training), 1983.
26. H. Levin and H. G. Schütze, "Economic and Political Dimensions of Recurrent Education", in Levin/Schütze (Eds.) *op.cit.*

Chapter VI
THE COSTS AND BENEFITS OF RECURRENT EDUCATION

1. *The Costs*

There has been much less attention paid to the costs of recurrent education, and the cost implications of moving towards such a system, than to the supposed benefits. Some of the literature suggests that it would not necessarily cost more than present systems, but would simply involve a redistribution of expenditure away from young people and in favour of older participants. Thus, the OECD analysis of trends and issues in recurrent education, suggests that "the current educational budget, as conventionally composed, should be analysed so that the proportional allocations made to youth and adult education are revelaed as clearly as possible, and from thos analysis there should follow policy decisions on the degree to which the proportion can and should be altered" (1).

However, the opportunity costs of educating older, experienced workers will always be greater than the costs of educating young people straight after compulsory education, since the earnings foregone by older workers exceed those of inexperienced school leavers. This means that the private opportunity costs are higher, since the individual must forego earnings in order to undertake education or training, and the social costs, in the form of lost production, are also higher. The benefits, moreover, of educating older workers will be delayed, and therefore the present value of these benefits is less than the present value of educating a young school leaver.

For this reason Stoikov argues that the costs of postponing higher education until after a period of employment are substantial: "The human capital losses in an option of 'postponement' of even as little as ten years are a very substantial portion of the capital value of the investment". He argues against postponement for this reason, although he also argues that the human capital losses of a policy of "investment in older individuals" are small compared to either the capital value of the investment or the losses involved in a system of postponed higher education (2). Thus, on cost grounds, Stoikov is against postponing higher education for more than five years, although he concludes that a policy of "second-chance" opportunities for older workers, which he describes as "investing in older individuals", is economically sound.

However, this analysis assumes that both younger and older people would be fully employed if they were not engaged in higher education, and both the costs and benefits are calculated on the basis of earnings differentials between workers with higher education and those with only secondary education. Since unemployment rates have been rising in most OECD countries in recent years, this will affect the opportunity costs of recurrent education and training. For the individual, the alternative to a course of education or training may be unemployment, and social security payments, rather than earnings from employment. In such cases, the cost, to the government, of providing social security payments should be deducted from the costs of providing education or training subsidies, whether in the form of grants to institutions, to cover tuition costs, or to individuals in the form of paid educational leave or training allowances.

Such a calculation may show that the extra costs of paying people to study rather than to be unemployed are minimal, which is why some economists advocate the use of social security payments to finance recurrent education. For example, Emmerij argues that in the Netherlands, it would be possible to provide paid educational leave for over 370 000 workers, as well as financing 350 000 students at present enrolled in post-compulsory education, at no extra cost to government funds. "In other words, close on 730 000 people in the Netherlands could make use of recurrent education through paid educational leave and receive between 75 and 85 per cent of their most recent income or a student salary. This would not represent a bigger financial outlay than is now found in the budget of the Ministry of Education and Sciences and of Social Affairs respectively" (3).

This sleight of hand consists of reclassifying government expenditure or, as Emmerij puts it, "instead of spending for *negative* reasons, the same amount of money should be used for *positive* reasons". However, it does not mean that the opportunity costs of recurrent education are zero, though it does mean they are lower than is often assumed. The costs of tuition, or training, will still be positive and may in some cases be higher for adults than for young people continuing their education straight after compulsory schooling. If the special needs of mature students require extra counselling services, or different teaching methods, then recurrent education may impose additional costs on institutions. On the other hand, the fact that adults already have work experience may mean that they are more highly motivated and learn more quickly than younger students.

Another factor that may reduce the costs of providing recurrent education or training is the existence of spare capacity in institutions due to demographic fluctuations. The fact that the number of school leavers will decline in many OECD countries in the late 1980s or early 1990s means that there will be spare capacity in many institutions, or redundant teaching staff and capital equipment, unless additional students can be enrolled from non-traditional sources (4). In other words, the marginal costs of enrolling these additional students in the future will be lower than average costs at present.

When all these dirrerent factors are taken into account, it is unrealistic to suggest that there would be no extra costs involved in moving towards a system of recurrent education, but these additional costs are likely to be lower than is sometimes assumed. How these costs would be shared between individual students or trainees, their employers and the government will depend on how recurrent education is financed.

At present, in most countries, governments finance a large part of post-compulsory education through institutional grants and financial aid to students, and most forms of initial vocational training are heavily subsidised. In some, such as Belgium, Sweden and Yugoslavia, initial training takes place in schools or other educational institutions. In other countries, such as Austria and the Federal Republic of Germany, a dual system of training means that both the costs and the provision of training are shared between employers and government, and even in countries such as Australia, Canada and the United Kingdom, where apprenticeship is important, and where employers provide and finance on-the-job training, there is a trend towards increasing the proportion of off-the-job training in institutions, which are heavily subsidised. Thus, in many OECD countries there has been a shift towards greater public financing for initial training, and the growth of public programmes of training and retraining for the unemployed in recent years has also meant an increase in the government's share. However, the bulk of in-service training is financed by employers or by trainees themselves, in the form of loss of earnings.

The way in which the costs of training should be shared between trainees, employers and government remains an unresolved question in several OECD countries. New mechanisms which were developed in the 1960s and 1970s for redistributing the costs of training, such as levy-grant systems, have not proved successful; other countries, such as France and Sweden, have introduced payroll taxes to help finance vocational training, while still others continue to subsidise training out of general taxation.

Unfortunately, economic theory does not provide an unambiguous answer to the question of how the costs of post-compulsory eduction and training should be shared between participants, employers and the state. Becker's famous distinction between general and specific training (5) was supposed to provide a guide for financing for vocational training, with trainees bearing the costs of general training, which would raise their productivity, and hence their earnings in many jobs, and employers bearing the costs of specific training. However, in practice the distinction between general and specific training often breaks down and whether or not training is specific often depends on conditions in the labour market as much as on the content of training (6). The economic argument for public financing of education and training rests on the importance of externalities, which means that the social benefits exceed the private benefits and therefore public subsidies are called for to prevent underinvestment. There are, of course, social arguments too, for public financing of education, for example, the need to ensure equality of opportunity and social cohesion. Economic analysis of methods of financing needs to be just as concerned with questions of equity as with efficiency.

However, although there has been considerable debate about the merits of different methods of financing post-compulsory education, there is no clear answer to the problem of how the costs should be shared between participants, employers and taxpayers. Neither on the basis of theoretical reasoning nor empirical evidence is it possible to make a definite judgement in favour of one or the other alternative. In other words, the costs of recurrent education will continue to be shared between governments, employers and participants, by a variety of financing mechanisms (7). The following chapter looks in more detail at various financing mechanisms that have been proposed.

However, first, we must turn to the question of whether the additional costs that would be incurred by moving towards a system of recurrent education can be justified, on strictly economic grounds. This depends on the magnitude of the benefits of recurrent education, either to the individual or to society, and to this topic we will now turn.

2. *The Benefits*

The standard way of measuring the benefits, or returns, to education is in terms of the additional lifetime earnings of educated people, and this is the way in which cost-benefit analysis has been applied to recurrent education by Stoikov (1975) and others (8). There is now a considerable literature on cost-benefit analysis of education which deals with the various objections that have been made to using earnings differentials as a measure of the returns to education (9). Although it remains controversial how reliable cost-benefit techniques are as a guide to resource allocation, any decision about whether to allocate additional resources to recurrent education will depend on perceptions of relative costs and benefits, even if these are not measured precisely in terms of rates of return. The benefits are not, of course, confined to purely economic benefits. One of the main arguments for recurrent education is concerned with social justice and the desire to achieve a more equal distribution of educational opportunities across generations. However, the question of economic benefits is important, and tends to dominate debates about whether or not there should be a shift in government expenditure to favour recurrent education.

If benefits are viewed entirely in terms of extra earning power, then the fact that older participants have a shorter remaining working life than those continuing their education immediately after school is bound to reduce the total lifetime benefits of education for older students. For this reason, the OECD proposal for a strategy of recurrent education in its Member countries argued that "a cost-benefit analysis based on classical economic considerations is bound to turn out to the disfavour of recurrent education", but suggested that "social goals such as equality, participation and benefit to the individual in terms of improved opportunities for his development" would outweigh this disadvantage (10). However, even economic benefits are not all fully measured by earnings differentials. In an attempt to catalogue all the benefits of higher education in the United States, Bowen produces a formidable list of direct and indirect benefits, many of which cannot be measured in monetary terms (11). However, most of the studies he cites are concerned with the benefits of conventional higher education, rather than recurrent education. It is important to establish whether there are any economic arguments that favour recurrent education for adults rather than the traditional "front-end" model of higher education. Two arguments are particularly important, that is that recurrent education can increase flexibility and overcome skill obsolescence among workers.

Recent technological developments make it more than ever necessary that the labour force should be flexible, in order to respond to changing patterns of demand, new production techniques and the need for new types of skill. Opportunities for older workers to update existing skills or acquire new ones therefore bring economic benefits as well as social ones. Stoikov examines arguments about the obsolescence of skills and human capital and argues that recurrent education and training are an important means of overcoming obsolescence, but he concludes that "the optimal role of recurrent education as an antidote for human capital obsolescence seems to be preventive rather than curative. Efficient programmes which would allow the non-obsolete individual to keep abreast of current technology are more attractive than attempts to isolate obsolete individuals and to enrol them in formal course work" (12).

This suggests that a strategy of recurrent education which provides opportunities for regular in-service training for employed workers will bring greater economic benefits than crash courses designed to retrain unemployed workers with obsolete skills, even though these are necessary at times of high unemployment. It can be argued, moreover, that neglect of recurrent training opportunities in the past has been one cause of the recent high rates of unemployment. Governments in several OECD countries are now giving greater emphasis to programmes which allow workers to update their skills. An example is the above-mentioned PICKUP scheme in the United Kingdom, which provides government subsidies for universities and colleges to offer more refresher courses for workers – Professional and Commercial Updating (the initials of which form the acronym). The British government believes that the responsibility for financing such training should lie with employers, but recognises the need for government initiatives to encourage provision of in-service training.

However, the provision of refresher courses for older workers will not necessarily redistribute education or training in favour of the least educated, even though Stoikov argues that "the poorer the educational background, the higher is the risk of obsolescence". This is because there is evidence from many countries that the workers who are most likely to benefit from on-the-job training or refresher courses are those who already possess skills and educational qualifications. Employers believe that a high level of general education improves the capacity to learn, and although it is sometimes argued that older workers lack this capacity, there is plenty of evidence that greater experience can more than compensate for any reduction in physical or mental powers (13). The fact that it is the more highly-skilled workers who are most likely to benefit from refresher courses means that recurrent education opportunities will tend to complement, rather than replace opportunities for initial education and training immediately after school.

Thus, Stoikov's analysis of the benefits, as well as the costs of recurrent education, leads him to support one strand of the recurrent education strategy, but to cast doubts on the other. He argues in favour of investing in older workers, whether by means of "second-chance" programmes, refresher courses or other means. However, he is much more sceptical of the benefits of postponement of higher education, so that an increasing proportion of young people acquire work experience before continuing their education.

One benefit that is sometimes suggested for postponement is that it would improve career choices if young people could gain work experience before making final choices about education, training and occupation. Recognition of the need to improve the career choices of young people has led to increased emphasis in some countries on guidance and counselling services as well as teaching about the labour market, and the characteristics of different jobs in the final years of compulsory and post-compulsory schooling, and opportunities for work observation or exploration in schools. Although such measures are important, the opportunity for young people to combine work and education and training, or the opportunity for older workers to enter the education system after work experience will also lead to more realistic and better informed career choices.

In fact, it is increasingly recognised that job choices cannot be made in terms of a once-for-all decision, any more than educational choices should be made in that way. Rapid technological changes mean that individuals may have to change jobs and even occupations several times during a working life, and recurrent education can help workers to be more flexible and adapt more quickly to changing economic conditions.

The early attempts to measure the economic benefits of education by means of the extra earnings of educated workers assumed implicitly that education made them more productive by providing knowledge and skills, but more recently economists have emphasised that the effects of education on attitudes, motivation and abilities may be just as important as the effects on knowledge and skills. Moreover, abilities such as communication skills may be just as important as cognitive skills or knowledge, and can be improved and developed through education and training. Similarly, flexibility and adaptability are qualities which may be developed through education, and will increase workers' productivity and earnings quite as much, in some cases, as technical knowledge or skills. By increasing the flexibility of older workers, recurrent education offers benefits both to the individual and to society.

3. *The Economic Justification for Recurrent Education*

The summary of costs and benefits so far presented shows that recurrent education clearly offers economic benefits, and changing technological conditions are likely to increase the benefits of some kinds of recurrent education in the future, such as refresher courses for older workers, while rising levels of unemployment have reduced the opportunity costs. Does this add up to an economic justification for switching to a recurrent model for post-compulsory education? To answer this question, it is necessary to return to definitions. Stoikov distinguished between investment in older people and postponement of "front-end" higher education. This is because it is much easier to justify the former, in economic terms, than the latter.

The economic case for providing education and training opportunities for older people is succinctly put forward by an industrialist who argues that in the future there will be major changes in the way work is organised, so that people will have greater leisure and greater freedom to choose when to work. He then goes on: "If one accepts the general sense of direction of this analysis, it brings together underused abilities, lack of training and a world of work where we will not only have more free time, but more control over how and when we take it. This brings me down firmly in favour of stimulating the demand for education to provide for missed opportunities and for changes through time in the attitudes of individuals towards education; education will also have an essential role in helping industry itself to cope with the demands of technological change. As an industrialist, it seems to me oddly illogical to suppose that a single dose of higher education from 18 to 21 could innoculate you for life. I therefore see the employment scene in the years ahead as supporting an expansion in educational opportunity, and I believe that a national economic case could be made out for this addition to educational provision, although the social case will stand on its own" (14).

The methods for achieving this which he proposes, include:

– To multiply the points of contact between educational institutions and people at work;
– To increase flexibility and local initiative;
– To maximise the ways into the system.

All these can be regarded as essential attributes of a recurrent model of education. However, this is clearly labelled an addition to educational provision, rather than a replacement for the traditional model. Of course, it is true that if post-compulsory education were organised in such a way as to maximise the points of entry, to encourage flexibility, for example, through more part-time study, and to provide financial or other incentives for older participants, it would radically change the existing system, which would no longer be dominated by the requirements of young people taking full-time courses immediately after school. However, in order to encourage participation by older groups, it is not necessary to deny opportunities to younger participants, particularly at a time of falling numbers in the traditional age groups.

The advocates of a radical transformation of traditional post-compulsory education, involving large-scale postponement of higher education for school leavers, do so because they believe that the myth that higher education is the prerogative of the young is too deep-seated to be dislodged without a transformation of the system, and the abolition of the "front-end" model. This line of reasoning may underestimate the extent to which the need for regular updating of skills is becoming recognised by employers and employees alike, and also the strength of the movement to bring theoretical teaching and work experience closer together during vocational education and training. If increasing numbers of young people receive combinations of education, training and work experience at the start of their working lives, either through initial training schemes, apprenticeships or through special programmes for the unemployed, then it will be more difficult to argue that education or training should be regarded as a "once-for-all" experience.

The economic justification for a flexible system of post-compulsory education is that economic and technological developments increasingly require a flexible labour force and population able to acquire and adapt new skills, knowledge and abilities. If the argument for recurrent education is presented in terms of a conflict between recurrent and traditional models, then it is necessary to justify spending additional resources to educate adults instead of young people. If, on the other hand, the argument is concerned with the way in which existing systems of post-compulsory education could be more closely co-ordinated and adapted in order to increase the opportunities and the incentives for experienced workers and other older people to participate in education and training, then the economic justification is stronger.

The Advisory Council for Adult and Continuing Education in the United Kingdom, for example, emphasized that what they are proposing is a co-ordination of existing provision, in order to create a coherent system from a fragmented one:

> In essence continuing education comprehends all the opportunities provided for the education and training of adults after they have completed their initial education at and immediately following school. To make a reality of this idea of education as a process continuing throughout life the present Council has advocated .... the development of a comprehensive system of continuing education. By that we do not mean another education sector to be set alongside school, further, and higher education: we do not mean creating another administrative division; we simply mean a conjunction of policies, provision, funding and attitudes, all of which make it increasingly possible for more and more adults to continue their education whenever, wherever and however their learning needs and demands are best met (15).

However, the strength of this argument is closely linked with the question of who should pay for these opportunities. Since recurrent education does comprehend so many different activities including vocational training, refresher courses and retraining, general education, and also remedial courses designed to overcome past educational inequalities or deficiencies (for example, adult literacy programmes), as well as leisure enrichment activities, it is unrealistic to expect a single model to be suitable for financing all types of recurrent education. The question of who pays must be closely linked with the question of who benefits, and this cannot be answered for recurrent education as a whole, but only for individual programmes or aspects of recurrent education.

It is, of course, necessary to ensure that the financing of recurrent education does not itself create a fragmentation of opportunities. One of the weaknesses of the present system of student aid in many countries is that it was designed to assist the "traditional" student entering higher education immediately after school, and now discourages participation by mature students (16). However, in order to overcome this it is not necessary to create a single system of student aid which gives the same degree of subsidy to all, regardless of age or type of education and training. That would make no economic sense. What is needed is a co-ordinated but flexible financing system, involving both public and private finance, grants and loans, employers' and employees' contributions, which would support a co-ordinated but flexible range of provision of recurrent education opportunities.

NOTES AND REFERENCES

1. OECD/CERI (1975), *Recurrent Education: Trends and Issues*, Paris.
2. V. Stoikov (1975), *The Economics of Recurrent Education and Training*, Geneva: International Labour Office, p. 16.
3. L. Emmerij (1983), in Levin/Schütze (Eds.), *Financing Recurrent Education –rategies for increasing Employment, Job Opportunities and Productivity*, Beverly Hills (Sage).
4. In fact it has been argued that "rescuing educational institutions" from the adverse effects of declines in enrolment is a powerful motive behind the opening of higher-education institutions to accommodate adults. See Levin and Schütze, "Economic and Political Dimensions of Recurrent Education", in Levin/Schütze, *op.cit.*
5. See G.S. Becker (1964), *Human Capital*, New York: Columbia University Press, pp. 11-18.
6. See M. Oatey (1970), "The Economics of Training with Respect to the Firm", in *British Journal of Industrial Relations*, Volume VIII, No.1.
7. See D. Timmermann, "Financing Mechanisms and their Impact on Post-Compulsory Education", in Levin/Schütze, *op.cit.*

8. See V. Stoikov (1975), opË cit., and K. Garricot (1972), "Recurrent Education: A Preliminary Cost-Benefit Analysis", *Occasional Papers*, No.6, Melbourne: ACER.
9. For a summary of the arguments for and against cost-benefit analysis of education, see M. Woodhall (1980), *Cost-Benefit Analysis in Educational Planning*, 2nd ed., Paris: UNESCO/IIEP; G. Psacharopoulos (1981), "Returns to Education: An Up-Dated International Comparison", in *Comparative Education*, Volume 17, No.3. See also A. Tuijnman (1986), *Recurrent Education and Socio-Economic Success: A Theoretical and Longitudinal Analysis*, Institute of International Education, Stockholm.
10. OECD/CERI (1973), *Recurrent Education: A Strategy for Lifelong Learning*, p. 69.
11. H.R. Bowen (1977), *Investment in Learning: The Individual and Social Value of American Higher Education*, San Francisco: Jossey Bass.
12. V. Stoikov (1975), *op. cit.*, p. 111.
13. This evidence is usefully reviewed by V. Stoikov (1975), *op. cit.*, pp. 37-43.
14. A. Cadbury, in O. Fulton (Ed.) (1981), *Access to Higher Education*. Guildford: Society for Research into Higher Education.
15. Advisory Council for Adult and Continuing Education (1982), *Proposals: The Case for a National Development Body for Continuing Education in England and Wales*. Leicester: ACACE.
16. For a discussion of the British system and its effects on mature students, see M. Woodall, "Financial Support for Students", in A. Morris and J. Sizer (Eds.) (1982), *Resources and Higher Education*, Guildford: Society for Research into Higher Education.

Chapter VII
FINANCING RECURRENT EDUCATION: PRINCIPLES AND MODELS

When reviewing existing obstacles to recurrent participation in education and training and ways to remove or lower them, finance proves to be a principal stumbling block. Even with existing systems of post-compulsory education and training we have seen (Chapter V) a number of instances of this – age ceilings for student support, the non-eligibility of part-time studies for financial support, the incompatibility of unemployment benefits and enrolment in full-time studies. All of these cripple the realisation of true recurrent education and training and impair individual flexibility and choice as to what and when to learn.

Educational finance is a common tool of educational policy making, and as such has a direct impact on the contents of programmes and the way they are delivered, the kind of providers and the degree of co-operation between them. From this, it would appear to follow that a financial system appropriate to recurrent education and yet acceptable nationally must meet a number of criteria already entrenched in the national scene. To test this proposition we have chosen four models for examination, each representing different mechanisms of finance and different sources of funding. Our purpose is not to advocate any one of them as the best suited for a system of recurrent education, but to identify elements of financing systems that appear to be conducive to a recurrent pattern of further study and professional training, equitable both with respect to access to post-compulsory education and with respect to the distribution of the financial burden. The outcome must, too, be efficient and feasible.

1. *Alternative Financing Models for a Recurrent Education System*

Although these four models are not the only options, they illustrate the wide range of possible ways of financing recurrent education that have been proposed in the literature. The term "model" implies that they are innovative blueprints, but some of their particular features are based on existing systems of finance. Their distinguishing feature is source of funds, thus:

- A proposal to finance post-compulsory education with publicly funded *individual entitlements*;
- *The concept of individual drawing rights* from a general income transfer insurance system;
- A system of financing recurrent education through *collective (parafiscal) funds* financed by a specific levy from employers;
- The provision of funds through (guaranteed income contingent) loans.

Within these basic models there is scope for considerable flexibility: each provides room for some degree of mixed funding. We will now describe the main features of each and, this done, analyse the implications for recurrent education.

Only one of the models ("entitlement") was specifically designed for recurrent education (1); the others were adapted either from general financing schemes or from particular branches within higher education. They must, therefore, be evaluated in more general terms.

a) *Financing Recurrent Education With Post-Compulsory Entitlements*

According to this proposal, government support of post-compulsory education and training would, for the most part, take the form of entitlements to individuals rather than grants to institutions that would then derive most of their income from fees.

Such an entitlement would mean that a guaranteed sum of money would be provided for each person eligible for education and training after their compulsory schooling. These entitlements could be used for a wide variety of educational purposes over a wide range of situations – universities, teacher-training colleges, short-cycle vocational courses, apprenticeships, on-the-job training, re-training programmes, and adult education (vocational and non-vocational). The course chosen might therefore have been sponsored by one of a variety of agencies – governments, non-profit bodies such as trade unions and religious institutions, as well as profit-seeking enterprises.

Any individual would be eligible for an entitlement upon reaching compulsory school-leaving age, provided that he or she enrolled in a programme that satisfied the criteria established by government. These criteria would relate to standards of financial accountability, content of the education and training, procedures for handling complaints from participants and the provision of accurate information about what was offered.

Entitlements would take the form either of loans or grants, and would be means tested against family income and other background characteristics of the student. In addition, the size of the entitlements would vary according to the type of training or education chosen, greater support being provided for study in fields that have a high school priority and unusually high costs.

According to this approach, the entitlement would be available to individuals over a long period of time, both prior to their entering the work force and during their working career. The entitlement account would accumulate interest to encourage the individual to consider carefully the recurrent and continuing education and training possibilities that will continue to exist over the life cycle. The individual could apply the entitlement to a university education or vocational training programme immediately following graduation from school but could, alternatively, defer its use for several years after leaving school.

The entitlements would be financed from public revenues. Levin argues in favour of the use of general revenue funds and suggests that income tax or some other broad-based tax, related to income, would be the most appropriate source of finance. He argues that income tax is progressive with respect to income and takes into account a number of sources of income, while a tax on labour earnings alone would unduly penalise the poor by not considering sources of unearned income such as rents, dividends, profits, and interest.

The prerequisite of such an entitlement scheme would be a comprehensive regulatory system and an information system. The main functions of a regulatory agency would include the following:

- Processing applications for entitlements and establishing the eligibility of the individual;
- Determining level and composition of entitlement for each individual applicant;
- Maintaining continuous and accurate records on the used and unused levels of the entitlements for each person and thus being aware of how much was still unallocated at any given time;
- The agency would be charged with monitoring and enforcement functions of various kinds, the most important of which would be the application and enforcement of eligibility standards for institutions and programmes (2).

Since an entitlement scheme places a heavy emphasis on alternatives and choice, an information system would be necessary to provide useful and accessible information for both the individual applicants and for all the bodies offering education and training. The kinds of information needed by the applicants would include programme descriptions, teachers' qualifications, curriculum, cost and size of course, facilities and placement services. Would-be participants might also be interested in the views of previous members of the course programme and the proportion of students who completed it.

The providing institutions would have to be informed as to eligibility standards for accreditation of programmes and courses under the entitlement scheme; student demand for particular types of programmes and, if possible, general trends relating to the take-up of different types of education and training by enrolment levels, costs, geographical distribution and changes in the patterns of these indicators from year to year. Finally, information to providers of services should include data on occupational trends (3).

In summary, this model is distinguished by government support of post-compulsory education and training being vested predominantly in individuals rather than in direct grants to *institutions,* the money coming from government tax revenues. It proposes a highly integrated system of finance whereby institutions would receive their funding via the fees of individuals. The entitlement may be entirely in the form of a grant or be composed of both a grant and a loan. If it were a mix of grant and loan, the balance could vary according to the individual's resources or his desired field of study. The scheme would cover a wide range of post-compulsory studies and training that conformed with requirements laid down by a government regulatory agency.

b) *Financing Recurrent Education Through a General Income-Transfer Insurance System*

The model of a general income-transfer insurance system which would give the individual "drawing rights" has not been developed specifically for recurrent education but as an overall plan for the regulation and allocation of work, study and leisure (including retirement). It is designed to allow for the greatest possible freedom of individual choice between work and the various types of non-work activity, including recurrent education and training:

> Freedom of choice in allocating periods of work study and leisure throughout the course of a lifetime presupposes the availability of a greater variety of patterns of working time and an apparatus for the transfer of liquidity (under risk-sharing insurance) between periods of directly productive work and other periods in each individual's life (4).

Advocates of such a system believe that it should be up to the individual to decide whether and when to interrupt work (or leave work in the case of early retirement) rather than having to comply with the standardised system which dictates and prescribes the age of retirement, the duration of annual vacations, and number of weekly working hours. Different forms of non-work time could thus become interchangeable according to the needs and propensities of the individual. It would be possible to choose between early retirement and study leave earlier in a career, for example, or between shorter weekly hours and longer annual vacations and a sabbatical leave. The choice would, of course, be limited by a ceiling of a maximum amount of non-work time, over the whole working life, and this would have to be continually reviewed to reflect such factors as increases in productivity. Such a limit would be based on existing provisions for non-work time such as annual holidays, retirement, sabbaticals, or paid educational leave schemes. But even within this ceiling the degree of freedom of choice and flexibility of work-time patterns might be limited for certain technical and managerial reasons.

The development of such a model for the allocation of time would require a single comprehensive financing system, which would integrate the present different income transfer schemes (such as paid educational leave schemes, retirement pensions and retraining funds) into one single income transfer system. This would finance all periods of voluntary or legally provided non-work. It would itself be financed along the lines of a social insurance system: contributions being made by both employers and employees, together with other social insurance fees, on the basis of a certain percentage of wages. The self-employed and those not gainfully employed could be included if the former contributed a proportion of their incomes into the fund while the government would finance contributions for the unemplyed, or those who, for equity reasons, should not be excluded, such as parents who stay at home to bring up children during part of their career or young men doing their military service.

All individuals would belong to the fund, as there would be general and compulsory membership for all citizens, who would be given the right to draw on the fund up to the limit of their actual or expected contributions. Thus the individual could overdraw in the beginning in anticipation of future contributions, but there would be an overall limit to the individual account which would also be used to finance an old age pension, after retirement.

With particular respect to education, the model provides "that the annual contributions in a general income-transfer insurance system are made high enough to cover not only the need for income during retirement and other leisure periods, but also the cost of a number of years of studies for everybody over and above their compulsory schooling; those who do not utilise this right at an early stage would have money available for study or leisure periods later in life or even as an improvement of their late income and retirement conditions" (5).

In addition to the possibility of taking one or several periods of non-work time during which income is paid from the insurance system, certain special financial incentives are suggested. This would include the provision of extra drawing rights if the individual uses them either at specific times or for specific purposes (e.g. during periods of slackening demand for labour for training for occupations in short supply). Although it is not explicit in Rehn's model, one could easily imagine the use of such incentives for education and training activities in general, i.e. the drawing rights would increase their value when used for these purposes rather than for leisure or early retirement.

The concept of individual drawing rights under a general income insurance system is the most far-reaching of the models discussed here because it addresses not only education but all non-work activities, and the relation between work and non-work for the individual. Nevertheless, its application to and use by the individual for recurrent education is obvious. The basic idea is that there should be a common system of income maintenance for the different periods of the individual's non-work time, including post-compulsory study and training periods, leisure time and early retirement. This unified system, it is argued, would give the individual much greater flexibility both in the timing and the use of non-work time and be less costly, less bureaucratic and more equitable than the separate funds and arrangements that now exist. It would be basically financed through employers' and employees' contributions along the lines of other social insurance schemes, but self-employed and persons not gainfully employed would be included.

The actual operation and distribution of the drawing rights could vary but a basic, fixed credit would be available to everyone at the end of compulsory schooling which would increase in value if the individual postpones further study at that stage, and would also increase in value if individuals chose to use them during periods of low demand for labour, or for retraining in the face of obsolescence and redundancy.

c) *Financing Recurrent Education by Collective (Parafiscal) Funds*

An alternative financing model is based on the idea of a collective fund, publicly administered, with recurrent education being financed through one or several parafiscal funds (6). These funds are autonomous membership corporations or foundations which are intermediate between strictly public bodies, and entirely private organisations (whether profit-making or not). The main characteristic of such an intermediate body is its relative autonomy in raising and distributing funds for an earmarked purpose and setting forth and monitoring the standards according to which the money is levied and distributed. The model would cover non-school-based training and continued education, both of a vocational and general nature, thus excluding traditional school and higher education. In other words, the general features of a model of parafiscal collective funds could be applied to the whole recurrent education system (7).

Some countries have applied the principle of collective parafiscal financing to the organisation of vocational education and, in particular, continuing vocational training and retraining. Examples include the Industrial Training Boards in the United Kingdom, and the Federal Employment Office in Germany (8). The exact features and degree of autonomy of parafiscal bodies differ, however, depending on their legal mandate. Likewise, levying revenues can take a number of different forms including levies from either employers, or employees, or both. Money from the public purse can also contribute so long as this does not alter the status of the parafiscal funds as autonomous bodies, raising the great bulk of their own revenues; this automatically limits the amount of contribution from general public revenues.

According to this model the money would be mainly levied from private and public enterprises, according to their ability to pay, and so neither individuals nor the public administration would be required to pay. However, it is suggested that the amount of public funds which at present finance the post-compulsory sector would instead flow into the collective fund, thus guaranteeing the fund a solid financial basis (9).

The calculation of the levy would be based on turnover, or profit, rather than on the payroll or the number of employees as a payroll tax would discriminate against labour-intensive enterprises and would speed up the process of substitution of labour by capital.

The fund would be administered by a central governing body and corresponding regional bodies. It would be governed by a board consisting of representatives of the federal and the state or regional ministries of education, and others from municipalities, as well as employer and trade union representatives and a number of independent experts in the field of continuing education and training, including academics and teaching and training personnel.

The central board would have jurisdiction, within legal limits, over the following matters:

- The uniform standard which would decide the amount of the levy required from each enterprise;
- The development of certain standards for the use and distribution of funds, based on criteria such as the content of eligible programmes, curricula, the professional qualification of teaching personnel;
- The monitoring of these quality standards, together with the regional organisations.

In addition to monitoring quality standards determined by the central board, the regional organisations would administer the distribution of funds in cooperation with a network of local agencies which would be charged with the actual handling of applications and payments. Both the central board and the regional agencies would be assisted by a number of committees, composed of employers and trade unions, and by expert advisory groups.

The fund, within this framework, would finance specific programmes and courses rather than give lump sum institutional grants. In principle, a variety of provision of programmes would thus be maintained. Where, however, the board felt that there was an undersupply (either geographically or otherwise) of programmes for which there was a demand, it could finance the establishment of public centres for recurrent education. These would be sponsored either by the municipalities or counties.

The fund would thus finance:
- The current costs of eligible programmes and courses. This would mean that individual participants would not pay tuition fees;
- Capital investment for public centres for recurrent education;
- Investment subsidies for non-public education and training institutions which could not be financed via the programme grants;
- Income maintenance for participants following full-time education or training. The amount of income maintenance would take account of the income of low-wage earners, though with a maximum ceiling (as under most social security systems).

In summary, this model has some clear distinguishing features. Its parafiscal nature – i.e. self-management and relative autonomy in raising and distributing funds – especially marks it off from the others under review. The source of the money would be mainly a levy on employers, or on both employers and workers, though there would be public contributions as well. As far as the individual participant is concerned, the fund would pay income maintenance (if taken during work time) and tuition fees, though unlike entitlements or individual drawing rights, the extent of an individual's rights to education and training and the degree of individual choice is not predetermined.

d) *Financing Recurrent Education Through (Income Contingent) Loans*

The idea of financing education through (guaranteed) loans is based on the following four premises:

- Individuals should pay for their own education as they derive financial benefits from it in the form of higher incomes;
- There is an educational "market" which works according to market principles: that is, consumers buy goods or services from enterprises; the consumer can choose among the offers of different providers of goods and services according to their needs and preferences; suppliers take account of these needs and preferences, thus producing goods and services at competitive prices;
- Since students from low- and medium-income groups are not able to pay the market prices for the educational services, these students should be enabled to borrow money in order to finance their education or training and repay later from their income;
- Since investments in human capital involve higher risks for the investor than other forms of investments (e.g. in machines or houses) the ordinary capital market would not, under normal circumstances, provide loans for education or training.

In order, therefore, for people to undertake recurrent education (i.e. invest in human capital) various government-supported loan programmes have been proposed. Although there are different models, they mostly follow the basic idea of an *Educational Opportunity Bank* which would lend money to post-secondary students, regardless of the student's resources. The loan would be calculated to cover tuition fees and subsistence costs. In exchange for the loan, the student would pledge a given percentage of annual income for a fixed number of years upon completion of his studies (10), thus making the system a self-sustaining one.

Although Income Contingent Loans have been suggested mainly for higher education, immediately after secondary school, the principle can be applied to other post-secondary education and training activities as well. This would have, however, important consequences for the modes and rates of repayment of loans as the number of years during which repayments are made will be affected by the borrower's age (11).

Therefore, if the basic concept of a loan programme for adults is a fixed-term repayment schedule, with the amount dependent or contingent upon future income, younger adults under the programme are indirectly subsidising older borrowers (on the assumption that repayments would not be made beyond the age of 65). In order to compensate for this, repayments at rates dependent on the borrower's age have been suggested, along the lines of life insurance plans, where repayments vary inversely with age: quite simply, the rates of repayment would increase with the age of the student (12).

The proponents of an income contingent loan scheme do not specify how much education or training would be financed by such a scheme. It must be assumed, however, that this amount depends on the market price of the courses of study, as well as the time available for repayment (13). Although it is not made explicit in the proposed schemes, it must be assumed that some kind of regulatory system would operate, which would 'accredit' eligible institutions or programmes, while the duration, type and quality of the educational programme is left entirely to consumer sovereignty.

Summing up: income contingent loans would enable recurrent students to borrow money from a government or otherwise publicly sponsored Equal Opportunity Bank for educational or training purposes. The loans would cover tuition fees, indirect costs as well as subsistence allowances. The interest rate would be subsidised and repayment rates would be fixed at a certain percentage of the individual's actual income thus making the rates "income contingent" and distributing the debt over a number of years. The choice of study or training programme would lie entirely with the individual. Several OECD countries have introduced student loan schemes for higher education (14). What is different about the scheme described here is that loans would be available to everyone as a right, subsidised and guaranteed by the government, to be used over the whole life cycle of individuals whenever they so choose, and repayment would be based on future income, whereas most existing loan schemes are "mortgage" type loans, rather than contingent on income.

2. *Criteria for Financing Systems Suited to Recurrent Education:*
   A Critical Appraisal

We can now proceed to analyse the models just described in the light of various efficiency and equity criteria. This will by no means be a complete exploration of all their merits and effects since this would need information about such imponderables as type of educational activity, size of programme, number of participants or duration and pattern of enrolment (15). Moreover, it is conceivable that a mix of sources of finance would provide a more feasible system than one relying purely on one model (16). Nevertheless, we have a clear enough picture by now to assess how well each would serve the aims and main policy objectives of a recurrent education system.

a) *Encouragement of the Recurrent Pattern*

Perhaps the most important criterion for judging these models is how far they actually allow or encourage a recurrent pattern of participation in education or training. All four permit some form of such participation, but each scheme would have its own implications.

Entitlements are deliberately designed to encourage postponement of participation since they would accrue interest thereby increasing their value the longer they are unused (17). Whether or not this would provide enough incentive to people to defer part or all of their education or training depends on a variety of factors, including the general labour market situation and how it affects the individual, e.g. whether he or she will have to accept or be prepared to accept, a poor job or even unemployment as a direct result of not continuing education or training.

The stimulation of recurrence in all non-work activities is an inbuilt and central feature of the general income transfer insurance scheme, especially if used as a countercyclical instrument in an active labour market policy when demand for labour slackens. It has been pointed out therefore that the value of drawing rights would have to be increased during unfavourable labour market conditions and for those who wish to obtain qualifications which are in emand in the labour market. Rehn has also suggested that the drawing right accrues interest the longer it is unused, as in the case of entitlements.

The collective fund, on the other hand, is intended for lifelong learning of different kinds and spread over the individual's entire lifetime. Therefore, this financing system includes income maintenance for participants during periods of either full-time or part-time study or training. However, there is no financial incentive to postpone further studies or training upon reaching compulsory school-leaving age. On the contrary, it is explicitly stated that income maintenance must be such as to serve as a disincentive to take up a job immediately, upon completing compulsory school (18). The idea is that people should complete a certain amount of post-compulsory education and still have the possibility to reurn later. It is the possibility of returning to education later in life, rather than the possibility of deferring further study or training at the end of compulsory schooling that is emphasized by the parafiscal financing model.

Financing recurrent education through income contingent loans is much more uncertain with respect to its incentive effects. Having been developed for the financing of higher education and then adapted and transformed into a financing scheme for recurrent education, it poses some basic problems. For example, income maintenance costs for adults are higher for 18 to 22 year-olds and repayment periods will be shorter, thus entailing higher rates of repayment. Therefore, a loans scheme may discourage, rather than encourage, a recurrent pattern of educational participation. Although this model may in principle be used for recurrent education, it is doubtful whether it would meet the criterion of encouraging, rather than simply allowing a recurrent pattern of participation.

b) *Promotion of Equality of Opportunity*

The second criterion for analysis of financing systems is how far the model schemes might be expected to enhance equality of educational opportunity (in terms of participation in post-compulsory education and training activities among different social groups).

It is well known that there are wide disparities in levels of educational attainments between the younger and older generations, on the one hand, and between different social groups, on the other. In order to increase equality between these different groups, educational opportunity has to be extended to those who, up to the present, have received least. This means that a scheme for financing recurrent education should be equalising in both intent and outcome. How do the suggested models meet this objective?

"To increase equity in the allocation of post-secondary education and training by assuring that the government provides equitable support for all eligible persons" is an explicit aim of the entitlement approach (19). Indeed, the idea that everybody should receive the same amount of money from the government for education or training upon completion of compulsory school while at the same time abolishing all other forms of public subsidies is fascinating in its simplicity and its seemingly straightforward approach to overcoming existing inequalities. However, even with the suggested modification which would differentiate between the needy and well-to-do students (the grant-loan mix of the entitlement) and according to the social value of the field of study (by which the amount of entitlement would vary), at least one major problem would be difficult to resolve by an entitlement approach. Since different kinds of education have different costs, this would mean that entitlement to equal amounts of money would not ensure access to equal amounts of education. The financial support needed by those who continue full-time school and go on to higher education will be considerably higher than for those who take up, and partly finance, an apprenticeship after the end of compulsory school, for instance, and then use their entitlement for evening courses or a few periods of educational leave of absence at a later stage. The cost, and therefore price differences between courses, are considerable.

The dilemma posed by this disparity in prices for different types of education thus consists in fixing the "right size" of entitlement. What the "right size" might be in cash terms depends on a number of factors and cannot be meaningfully discussed out of the context of a concrete national system. But it would probably be difficult to steer clear of either underfunding the entitlement (which would mean that higher education students would need additional resources) or overfunding it, thus leaving a sizeable part of the entitlement unused in the case of students in other types of education. In the former case, it would add additional inequality to the existing disparities as only students from well-to-do backgrounds would be able to top up their entitlements and pursue university studies. In the latter case – provided this could be financed at all – many individuals would probably not use up all of their entitlement for educational purposes.

Were this to happen, Levin has suggested that unused balances should be refunded to the individual at retirement age or given to his estate in the case of early death. While this might be considered equitable, it would provide no incentive to use the entitlement money for education or training, at least not for low-income earners. It is precisely this section of the population who receive the lowest retirement benefits and who would thus be inclined to use their entitlements to secure an acceptable standard of living after retirement. As this is the group who have normally had the least education, the possibility of choosing between education and capitalisation of unused entitlements upon retirement appears to pose considerable problems.

There are two separate problems to be resolved, namely how to provide income maintenance and how to finance tuition. The concept of drawing rights would increase freedom of individual choice in allocating non-work time by providing some income maintenance during sizeable periods of study or training. Although income maintenance may be the largest financial cost of recurrent education, the question of how to finance tuition is also important. Although there are some OECD countries where certain types of education are provided free or practically free of charge, there are other sorts of education and other countries where tuition fees are significant. Therefore, students would presumably have to continue to rely on either family support, savings, scholarships or loans in order to be able to afford to use their non-work time for education or training. If annual contributions to the insurance system must be high enough to cover the cost of a number of years of study this would mean very high levels of contribution in cases where tuition fees are paid by the student.

Parafiscal schemes of the kind suggested would take care of both income maintenance and tuition costs during periods of study or training so that no financial contribution of participants in recurrent education activities would be required. It cannot, however, be firmly established whether this mode of finance would lead to an expansion of recurrent education opportunities, before it is known how much would be made available to individual students.

Income Contingent Loans would extend opportunities to those who would not be able to pursue further studies or training if they had to rely solely on family support or their own savings, but it is sometimes suggested that loans would discourage participation by low-income students. Another problem is that in many countries academic higher education is heavily subsidised from public funds, whereas opportunities for recurrent education may receive lower subsidies. It would give rise to considerable inequities if students relied on loans to finance recurrent education, while students in full-time higher education received grants or free tuition, particularly since higher education students tend to come from higher-income groups.

c) *Motivation of Disadvantaged Groups*

One of the main objectives of recurrent education is to motivate and enable disadvantaged groups, particularly those who have low incomes or are poorly educated to return to education. Any system of finance that aims to achieve this objective would have to give specific economic incentives to these groups. Let us see how the four models approach this problem.

The entitlement scheme would address it by giving grants to these groups while better-off students would receive repayable loans only. A cash subsidy with no concomitant financial obligation on the part of the recipient is certainly a considerable incentive to use it for education. However, if it were possible to use the cash for topping up pensions instead of for education this would act as a disincentive and run counter to the attempt to attract this particular group into education.

The drawing rights scheme is somewhat unclear about the value and size of the specific incentives to be given to "those who are not spontaneously motivated and attracted to studying". Since the scheme has been primarily designed as a general income-transfer system, and as an instrument in an active labour market policy, the principle of equality of educational opportunity and positive discrimination in favour of the disadvantaged is not a major priority of this scheme. The original model compares two strands of economic thinking. On the one hand, it concerns theoretical principles: how are the marginal benefits from studies (a mixture of consumption and investment) shared as between the individual, his employer, and society as a whole, and how therefore should the costs be allocated in order to lead to the best use of resources and to encourage citizens in desirable numbers to prefer studies to doing nothing? On the other hand, it is a practical question of experimentation and experience: how big do the contributions of the state have to be, during different conjunctural situations and in different sectors of the economy, in order to maximise the societal benefits, for example, through the decision of a desirable number of workers to use their study rights during a slack period and to train themselves for shortage occupations? (20)

Thus, if individuals would be more likely to use their drawing rights for purposes other than education (for example, leisure activities), then it would be necessary for these rights to have a higher value if used for educational purposes in order to promote and encourage recurrent studies and training. But this raises a number of further questions. How would such incentives be financed and who would decide about the size of incentives? Would such incentives be given to everyone who opts for education or training rather than for leisure-type activities, or would additional incentives be confined to those with low previous education?

All in all, it is probably fair to say that a self-contained system of income transfer payments financed by contributions from employers and employees would probably not provide any specific financial incentive for the low motivated to use their entitlements for education as this would not be compatible with the principle of a social insurance system. If there were to be financial incentives, therefore, they would have to be financed from outside the scheme, probably from public funds, since it is not feasible to expect members of an insurance scheme to subsidise special groups by increasing the value of their drawing rights at the expense of their own.

As far as the parafiscal scheme of financing is concerned, there appears to be no explicit provision for special incentives for the disadvantaged. The answer to this question would be left to the self-management of such collective funds, together with all questions of eligibility and content. Since the governing bodies of parafiscal schemes will be composed of different parties, including the representatives of the state, it might be expected that particular attention would be paid to those groups with a low educational background and appropriate arrangements made to attract them through specific incentives, but this is not a necessary feature of a collective fund.

The concept of income contingent loans is based on the idea that, under the normal conditions of repayment of "mortgage"-type loans, the inherent riskiness of the return from the individual investment would discourage potential participants from investing in education. It is assumed, however, that an individual might be prepared to borrow if it were a contingent repayment loan, meaning that if income is low, repayment rates are small. It is argued that this would be particularly true in the case of the poor, who would not be obliged to repay the full amount of the loan if they did not succeed with their studies or if their salary were not sufficiently high. In other words, the loan would be repaid in full only by those who derived financial benefits from their investment, in the form of higher lifetime income (21).

The hard fact remains, however, that borrowing money, even under favourable conditions, means having to repay it, either in part or in full. It is hard to see how individuals will be motivated to borrow to invest in their own education if they either do not believe in the value of education at all or if their previous experience with education was such they they do not expect to succeed in any educational programme. Therefore, opponents of loans argue that any form of loan would act as a disincentive to disadvantaged groups, and that only grants would provide sufficient incentive to persuade them to invest in recurrent education. On the other hand, experience with student loans for higher education shows that some low-income students are willing to borrow to finance their education, particularly when the loan repayment terms are favourable. The question is whether loans would provide sufficient incentive for investment in all forms of recurrent education, or whether they would be used only for vocational education offering high returns.

d) *Parity of Treatment between General and Vocational Education*

In principle, all of the four financing models cover financial support for education and training ranging from general and completely non-vocational to directly vocationally-oriented training activities. However, there are certain differences in emphasis. The entitlement approach proposed by Levin was, in an earlier and more elaborate version, limited to career preparation and its scope was only later broadened to include non-vocational activities (22). Rehn's drawing rights model tends to emphasize vocational education through the use of additional financial incentives for vocationally-oriented education and for retraining activities. The parafiscal model probably best meets this criterion of parity since it would not only try to ensure parity between general and vocational education but also a better co-ordination and eventually integration of the different sectors. The aim of parafiscal funds would be to ensure that representatives of different spheres of interest were involved in the organisation of the fund, so that all post-compulsory education and training provision could be co-ordinated (23). Since income contingent loan schemes have been primarily advocated for higher education, the emphasis is mainly on the vocational component of education since there is the underlying assumption that investment in education will yield an increase in income from which the loan can be repaid. This, it can be argued, would be essentially limited to educational programmes which are recognised to have a direct professional relevance while general education might be neglected by the students. It may even be that the Lending Bank would encourage the tendency since the higher the level of future income, the greater the monetary returns to the Bank from income contingent repayments.

e) *Equitable Distribution of Financial Burden*

Although the four models all share certain features, they differ with respect to sources of revenue. However, two of the schemes suggest variations to meet equity considerations.

For example, it is proposed that entitlements take account of differences in family resources and background by distinguishing "grant" entitlements and "loan" entitlements. The former would go to needy students and the latter to the student from higher-income families, with various combinations of loans and grants for intermediate groups. The justification for differentiation according to the financial need of the individual student is that wealth and income are unequally distributed and the notion of equity requires unequal and not identical treatment. Likewise, it has been proposed that income contingent loan schemes be complemented by grants to needy students and that the size of the grant should depend upon the size of the family income. How far either "loan entitlements" or mixed "grant-loans" of this kind could be extended before they became inconsistent with the basic principles and approach of the scheme concerned is a moot question (24). In fact, given these suggested modifications of the principles of both models, it is hard to see in what respect the two modes of financing are really different, since both entail individual support of students by a means-tested combination of loans and grants.

The basic principle of both models is that individuals should pay for their own education provided they can do so, thus combining the he-who-benefits-should-pay and the ability-to-pay principles. Nonetheless, everyone would be eligible for at least a loan (to be repaid from later income) thus helping students from well-to-do backgrounds to establish independence from their family resources and creating, in the words of one, "a modicum of equity" (25). Needy students would receive either a grant or a subsidy composed of a mixed grant and loan – according to the student's family resources. This system resembles in principle existing student support systems for higher education in several OECD countries (26).

The discussion cannot, however, be left there. The special characteristics of recurrent education raise some important issues. Firstly, since recurrent education is for adults, up to what age can family (i.e. parents') resources be taken into account? While it may be reasonable to take account of parents' income in determining aid for young people who attend university in direct continuation of secondary school, it appears nonsensical with respect to adults. Therefore, any means-testing would have to be based upon the potential student's own resources. But this raises another problem. Apart from students with substantial capital, property or savings, or those who are entitled to paid sabbaticals or to educational leave of absence, most adults would have no source of income if they gave up paid employment for full-time study, so would have no income on which means-testing could be based. It is possible that it might be based upon income from previous work (assuming the individual has worked before), though this may well be already spent and thus no longer at the student's disposal.

Secondly, the fact that recurrent education is for adults raises problems with any financing system involving loans. The basic assumption of a loans scheme is that, under normal circumstances, the investment will have adequate returns and that therefore the borrower will be able to repay the loans – that is, that the education will actually lead to a greater income. Although this may be a reasonable expectation for young people, it is certainly problematic for older people where the time span for repayment is shorter than in the case of young people. This represents an important disincentive to postpone periods of education and follow a recurrent pattern of education spread over an entire lifetime. This problem has often been raised as an economic argument against recurrent education, judged in terms of cost-benefit analysis. The opportunity cost of investing in education is greater for older than for younger people, that the older person had the option of postponing education (27). A self-contained financing system based on individual loans for educational activities must necessarily be concerned to ensure that loans are in fact paid back. It is, therefore, hard to see how an Educational Opportunity Bank or any other income contingent loan scheme would be capable of enabling individuals to pursue full-time education at a later stage in their lives, rather than in direct continuation of compulsory schooling. This alone is a very serious limitation of the loan model.

The drawing rights model raises different but equally important issues with respect to the equity criterion. Unlike most social insurance systems for sickness or work accidents, the payments the individual would receive from the fund would be based on normal wages or salary. In this respect, the model resembles pension funds rather than sickness compensation. Existing differences in wages and salaries would thus continue during the periods of non-work. While this may be thought acceptable as far as income maintenance is concerned, it clearly influences the individual's ability to pay for tuition and incidental expenses associated with education, such as travel, books, tools, arrangements for child care. Unless tuition is either free or there are additional subsidies for those in middle- or lower-income brackets to cover other expenses, the system would put an inequitable financial burden on low earners.

The proposed parafiscal model avoids this kind of problem by covering all costs, including income maintenance, tuition and incidental costs. However, as noted above, the parafiscal model does not embrace the higher-education sector, which would continue to be funded entirely or in part from general tax revenues, according to the systems of OECD countries. Thus the problem of unequal allocation of educational resources between the sectors and of inequitable distribution of the overall financial burden between different groups would continue to exist. Thus, in order to abolish existing inequities caused by different financial arrangements for different types of post-compulsory education, the parafiscal model would have to be expanded in scope to cover the entire post-compulsory sector, including higher education.

This raises the question of whether there is any justification for financing compulsory education, general post-secondary education and recurrent education differently. All OECD countries provide compulsory education free of charge, and provide substantial subsidies for higher education, though in a variety of ways, including the provision of free tuition, grants or scholarships to individuals, subsidised student loans or a mixture of various forms of student aid. In most countries, the degree of subsidy for recurrent education is much less. One reason why governments subsidise compulsory and general post-compulsory education is that they recognise that investment in education generates benefits to the whole of society, and not just to the educated individual. However, the difficulty of defining and measuring with any accuracy the benefits of education means that "he-who-benefits-should-pay" does not provide a clear-cut guide to how the costs of education should be distributed between individuals and the general taxpayer. In the case of recurrent education, it is clear that there are benefits – both economic and social – that accrue both to the individual and to society at large, so that the benefit principle does not demonstrate how the costs of the education should be shared.

It is therefore sometimes argued that the benefit principle should be replaced by the principle that the financial burden of education should be distributed according to individual ability to pay. However, it is not clear that this would lead to greater equity in the distribution of costs and we have suggested above, that in the case of recurrent education it is often difficult to define "ability to pay".

f) *Flexibility and Individual Freedom of Choice*

Rehn's concept of a general income insurance with individual drawing rights aims explicitly at "the greatest possible freedom of individual choice"; in fact, he argues emphatically that it would lead to "a society of free choice" (28). As originally put forward this freedom refers to the allocation of time for work, study and leisure; but we have just seen that it can as well refer also to the possibility of choosing freely between different types of educational activity. As the drawing rights model is not primarily concerned with recurrent education, it must be assumed that the individual choice is limited to the range of choice traditionally available, i.e. within the provision of existing education systems.

It is argued that this matter of availability would be quite different under the proposed entitlement system. The "consumer" would not only be able to choose freely between existing types of provision but also, through the choice exercised in deciding where to spend entitlements, the individual would be able to influence the provision itself. As institutions providing education and training services would rely financially on entitlements from students enrolling in their programmes, the contents of the programmes offered would probably adapt to individual demand to a large extent. But the implications for freedom of choice might not be all positive. Institutions would probably respond most obviously to popular demand, or to that of the "average consumer", which would thereby secure them the greatest amount of resources in the form of entitlement money. This might encourage institutions to drop most of those programmes and services that attract only a few students and are thus not profitable. Other than under the present system of mixed public and private provision of post-compulsory education, it might well be expected that institutions would no longer serve the marginal student, taking less common subjects and courses, as they would have to compete with the private sector for students' fees and would thus be compelled to shape their supply according to the demands of the majority. Therefore, the entitlements scheme might well have the effect of significantly reducing the range from which the student has to choose.

Concerning the proposed parafiscal schemes, it appears that individual choice would to a large extent depend on the eligibility criteria for education and training programmes which would be established by the governing body(ies). However, it can be expected that the composition of these boards, reflecting a variety of interests, would assure a large variety in the eligible programmes. The fact that the decisions of these boards concerning eligible programmes would have to be agreed upon by representatives of three different spheres of interest (government, employers, unions) as well as by educational experts, makes it very unlikely that programmes would be neglected if either one or other of these parties deemed them to be important. In addition, the envisaged system aims at a better and more equitable geographical distribution, and hence access to programmes and services, which is an important factor in broadening and guaranteeing freedom of choice.

What has been said for entitlements would basically apply also to income contingent loans as both modes of financing would rely on the mechanisms of the market, rather than on any kind of educational planning, although of course the proposed accreditation of programmes under the entitlement scheme is a kind of planning instrument. However, the basic idea behind financing education through loans is the belief that this investment in education will pay out in terms of (and be repaid from) higher incomes later on. This implies a close scrutiny by the individual (and presumably by the Bank as well) as to whether or not participation in the intended education or training programme can be reasonably expected to lead to a higher income from which the borrowed money can be repaid. If this does not take place, it is probably fair to assume that this would lead students to put an emphasis on those programmes which are more or less vocationally-oriented, thus narrowing students' choice to programmes which can be expected to have direct payoffs in professional or employment terms.

There is another important issue that must be raised when discussing individual flexibility and freedom of choice. Both the entitlement and the loans from the Educational Opportunity Bank schemes would give the individual a certain amount of money (either as a grant or a loan) to be used at any time between compulsory school-leaving age and retirement. Although there would be some kind of an information and regulatory system, the principle is that it is the individual who makes the decision as to the timing and the kind of programmes followed. Likewise, under the drawing rights model, it is individuals who decide at which point they want to use their drawing rights. Although this kind of individual choice and self-determination can well be considered an asset, it should not be overlooked that it also puts a considerable onus on the individual, who would have to decide at the age of eighteen, for example, whether to borrow a major sum of money, under an income contingent scheme, to finance education which, at a later stage in a working life, might no longer appear as valuable or meeting professional or personal needs. It also generates debt for the rest of a working life and excludes the possibility of taking up education or training later. The student's freedom of choice can thus turn out to be a burden, if there is no possibility of reversing decisions already taken and especially for those, often with less education, who tend to be less informed about the world of education, and may well make choices they would want to change later on when the entitlement or loan or drawing rights account is already used up. Thus, it must be noted that this much cherished idea of freedom of choice, particularly as viewed by liberal economists, is not without serious drawbacks. While it may be said that this risk is not unlike that which any consumer faces in a free market system, it is not ordinary merchandise, but education, which is at stake.

g) *Feasibility and Efficiency*

Much can be said about the feasibility and efficiency of the proposed systems. Given the obvious need for brevity, the discussion in this section will be centered around the single, but very large issue of whether it is feasible to finance recurrent education by these means.

Any discussion of how the proposed model schemes can be financed cannot avoid addressing the question – "How much would they cost?". It was mentioned above that an answer not only depends on a number of variables (some of which, like levels and patterns of participation, would themselves be greatly influenced by the availability of finance and the ways in which the money could be used), but that it would also have to take into account numerous trade-offs with other parts of the education sector as well as with other policy sectors which would be affected. Having said this and remembering the general caveat that finance can only be concretely discussed in relation to specific programme activities, we can, however, try to outline some of the considerations bearing on the question of whether these models are actually financially feasible.

The Educational Opportunity Bank scheme is probably the easiest to tackle. Since its underlying principle is that individuals pay for their own education, while the state continues to subsidise the education sector by grants to institutions, the system would be basically self-contained, requiring relatively small additional public funds only to subsidise the interest on the loans and any additional subsidies were grants to be given to needy students (29).

It is less clear what the financial implications of the drawing rights model would be. As a general principle, the system relies on contributions from employers and employees in a similar way as social insurance funds (such as health or unemployment insurance). Yet, in spite of this similarity, it is not insurance in any normal sense, as it is based on the idea of a comprehensive account of individual rights to paid non-work time, rather than on a contingency (like sickness, accidents at work or unemployment) or a certain event (such as reaching retirement age).

It would cost no more than under present arrangements only if the total amount of salaried non-work time available to draw upon did not exceed the sum of paid periods of voluntary and age-determined non-work time under existing provisions (for example, annual leave, paid educational leave or sabbaticals, temporary or old age retirement).

But in this case, the system seems to boil down to little more than providing greater flexibility to the individual to decide when to use his or her non-work time. Desirable as this may be, it is certainly questionable whether this would provide sufficient basis for all post-compulsory education and training requirements (especially if it is full-time) and it is even more questionable whether the individual would want to use a sizeable part of his accumulated non-work time for these purposes. It is also to be wondered in this case why people should want to contribute financially to this kind of scheme, since it would replace a system where employers pay for much of existing non-work provision with one where individuals make a significant contribution themselves.

It seems likely, therefore, that this scheme would only work if it allowed for a real increase in aggregate non-work time, over and above, that is, the sum total presently available. For this to be possible, additional funds will be required. These funds, in line with the drawing rights principle, would come from employers and employees and/or government subsidies. If they were to come from employers and employees, it would raise problems, since already the size of social security contributions are a subject of primary concern in most of those OECD countries which operate systems of this kind. If employers and employees were expected to pay contributions over and above present levels, the feasibility of the scheme would be in question, not only because employees already pay substantial contributions but also because it would add to the costs of labour which, in turn, could have a negative influence upon employment.

The results of a recent enquiry by the Dutch Committee on Paid Educational Leave of Absence are, however, worth noting in this context. This Committee, charged by the government to look into the costs and modes of financing of a paid educational leave of absence scheme, recommended its introduction to be financed partly from social insurance funds and partly by government subsidies. In recommending the use of social insurance funds, an important consideration was that these funds (unemployment and health insurance) already have to support some of the costs of structural unemployment through the payment of benefits. Many of those for instance who are sick or classified as "unfit for work", so the Committee argued, could equally be classified as unemployed. Therefore, in recommending the use of social insurance funds, it was thought that educational leave of absence would be both more constructive and actually shorten the period of a person's dependence on benefits in the longer term. In conclusion, the Committee proposed that such a scheme should be financed from public funds (including social security funds), through a redeployment of resources and indeed suggested that few, if any, additional funds would be required (30).

Since it has been suggested that additional non-work time, and hence resources, would be necessary to make the drawing rights scheme workable, and having discussed some considerations of using social insurance funds, we can turn to the second alternative – government subsidies. These would come either from general tax revenues (and thus compete with other policy sectors for scarce resources) or, where possible, from special earmarked taxes for education and training. In either case, it seems unlikely that governments would finance extra non-work time to be spent as the individual chooses, but would probably only provide the additional resources if they were to be used for education or training purposes. Whether it would cost more or not is another question since the money might come from a redeployment of existing resources. It is not unreasonable to propose that both the "front-end" educational system would require fewer resources and that money otherwise used to bear the costs of unemployment might be channelled into paying for the drawing rights scheme. Since the conclusion of this discussion is that it seems unreasonable to expect that governments would agree to put additional finances into the funds for drawing rights unless it were to be used for specific purposes such as education and training, then it undermines the main principle of this model – that it is the individual who chooses when and how to use the rights to which he or she is entitled. Moreover, if it is correct to think that additional resources would be made available only for specific and designated purposes, then this raises the question of whether there is any real distinction, in principle, between the drawing rights scheme under these conditions, and the situation which prevails in OECD countries at present.

Turning now to entitlements, the distinction must be made between entitlements as loans and those as grants. The question and issue of feasibility of loans has already been discussed in relation to income contingent loans and it is not necessary to repeat it again. Entitlements as grants would be financed from general tax revenues, preferably, it is suggested, from income tax. This immediately raises the question, is it feasible to raise income tax to meet this new demand for resources and what would be the scale or order of magnitude of the funds required?

Again, it is difficult to decide on the order of magnitude since so much depends on how far resources would be redeployed and the trade-offs available with existing expenditure. The entitlements scheme, it must be remembered, proposes to absorb all other arrangements for financing post-compulsory education, into its orbit. Concrete consideration of the scale of resources required is additionally complicated since it is extremely difficult to assess realistically even the present scale of public support to post-compulsory education which, in any case, varies considerably from country to country.

It seems most useful, therefore, to consider the figures and estimates which Levin puts forward. His starting point was the estimate that the State of California subsidised publicly financed four-year colleges at that time by about $2 500 per student a year in the early 1980s (thus making $10 000 per student for the four years). This provides the basis for the estimated size of his entitlement. However, to this would have to be added a sum covering living expenses. $500 a month, being roughly equivalent to the official poverty line, cannot be considered an over-generous allowance and so it could be used as a minimal estimate for living expenses. Therefore, $6 000 can be added to the $2 500 basic entitlement. A third component should be taken into consideration, i.e. what is presently paid by students to colleges as tuition fees. $1 000 to $1 500 a year was probably a fair (minimum) estimate of tuition fees, so that the total per year would come to $10 000 (2 500 + 6 000 + 1 500). Since the entitlements scheme as proposed by Levin is based on the idea that everyone would have the right to follow the four-year course or its equivalent, this made the total entitlement $40 000 for each student. Even recognising that a certain proportion of this would be in the form of loans, it seems safe to say that if everyone were eligible to this sum or its equivalent in current prices, the total outlay would far exceed the present total public support for post-compulsory education. Even these very rough estimates, therefore, indicate that the aim of giving everyone the money to undertake four years of university education or its equivalent, however laudable in many respects, is bound to be financially more expensive than the present system.

A more realistic example may thus be a one-year entitlement for education and training. Even with this example, the costs are likely to remain high. In a 1976 OECD report (31), model calculations were made on the assumption that all employed people would have one year during their career for recurrent education, and they would be paid their full salary during this time. The estimates suggested that it would cost between one and a half and two per cent of GDP (32). The report does indicate that it would be less expensive if, as seems plausible, not everyone took up their right to study leave or if ways were found of paying people somewhat less than their full salary. It should, however, be noted that the non-use of the entitlement would not reduce the costs of the scheme as outlined by Levin; it would simply mean it would be paid to him/her upon retirement or it would go to his estate in the case of premature death (33).

We have thus considered a number of factors that would influence the likely scale of costs of the entitlements scheme. The speculative question – would the considerable additional public funds required to finance even a modest entitlements scheme be forthcoming – has not yet been directly addressed. However, given the commitment of many governments to reduce public expenditure, and given the resistance of taxpayers to continued increases in personal taxation, which led to the much publicised "Proposition Thirteen" in the State of California some years ago, it can no longer be assumed that increased public finance for such a scheme is feasible.

Turning now to the last of the four model-financing systems, the parafiscal model: since public financial support would not be any higher than at present and would be paid into the parafiscal fund as a grant, then any increase in the post-compulsory sector would have to come through the enterprise levies. It is again open to speculation whether industry can be expected to bear the burden of the costs of an expanded recurrent education system. Whatever the answer to this question, there are a number of more specific issues which merit attention.

The size of the levies would depend upon the net profits of the enterprise, which raises the question of what would happen during periods of recession and low economic performance. This question has not gone unnoticed and it has been suggested that economic fluctuations would be met by borrowing money on the capital market during recessions, which would be repaid when economic performance is high (34). (Clearly this depends on confidence in the cyclical nature of economic change.) It is true that collective funds such as pension schemes do indeed follow this practice, though it needs also to be said that such funds are usually less sensitive to the twists and turns of economic performance than a fund based on net profits.

We have already mentioned that costs which are borne by enterprises may be passed on to the consumer by means of higher prices, or the worker, through induced wage reductions. It is possible that this would be more difficult with a levy based on profits than on the payroll or turnover (35). Whilst this would follow the intention of the financing scheme, the question then is raised of the extent to which such a levy would operate as a disincentive to making and showing profits and the resistance it would encounter (36). General answers to these questions are impossible to suggest in the abstract but such a consideration should be taken into account in discussing its feasibility.

Whether the additional funds for recurrent education under a parafiscal scheme could be raised through levies on enterprises is far from dependent, therefore, solely on the size of the levy. There is a complex of factors at play. Moreover, the influence of enterprises, if they were expected to foot the bill, on the content of the education and training should not be overlooked. It again seems plausible that they will more readily participate in such a scheme, the more that the education and training is seen as meeting their own requirements and interests, and the higher the expected return, in the form of increased productivity.

3. Envoi

To try and draw the strands of this chapter together in a series of neat recommendations and suggestions would contradict one of the basic thrusts of the previous pages. There are too many areas and issues which have as yet received far too little attention to enable final or sweeping conclusions to be drawn. In particular, no single one financing system emerges as the "ideal" one for a system of recurrent education and the above models could serve as elements in a mixed financing system that would have to take into account the respective structures, traditions and patterns of finance of post-secondary education and training existing in OECD countries. The foregoing analysis of the implications of alternative financing models may then provide some indication of how well different systems of financing would meet the fundamental objectives of recurrent education.

NOTES AND REFERENCES

1. There is a substantial body of literature about different types of entitlement schemes. Cf. H. Levin, "Individual Entitlements", in H. Levin/H. G. Schütze (Eds.) (1983), *Financing Recurrent Education – strategies for Increasing Employment, Job Opportunities and Productivity*, Beverly Hills (Sage), pp. 39-66; and in: D. Kuhlenkamp and H. G. Schütze (Eds.) (1983), *Kosten und Finanzierung der beruflichen und nichtberuflichen Weiterbildung* (Cost and Financing of Continuing Education), Frankfurt (Diesterweg). Cf. also Norman Kurland (Ed.) (1977), *Entitlement Papers*, Washington D.C. (National Institute of Education).
2. Cf. H. Levin, in Levin/Schütze, *op.cit.*
3. *For further details, see Levin, in Levin and Schütze, op.cit.*
4. "Individual Drawing Rights" in Levin and Schütze, *op.cit.*; and "Die Finanzierung der periodischen Weiterbildung durch ein System individueller Ziehungsrechte" (Financing Recurrent Education Through a System of Individual Drawing Rights), in Kuhlenkamp and Schütze, *op.cit.*; cf. also

Gösta Rehn (1978), *Towards a Society of Free Choice*, holm (Swedish Institute for Social Research); translations: *Vers une société de libre choix*, Droit Social, No. 7/8 July/August 1978; and *Die Gesellschaft der freien Wahl*, in Festschrift für Elisabeth Liefmann-Keil, Berlin (Duncker & Humblot), 1978.

5. G. Rehn (1978), in Levin/Schütze, *op. cit.*, p. 141.
6. Cf. Friedrich Edding (1974), "Educational Leave and Sources of Funding" in S. Mushkin (Ed.), *Recurrent Education*, Washington D.C. (National Institute of Education); and Friedrich Edding, Ulrich Boehm, Gisela Dybowski, Hedwig Rudolph (1976), *Struktur und Finanzierung der Aus- und Weiterbildung* (Structure and Financing of Initial and Continuing Education and Training), Göttingen (Schwarz).
7. Werner Clement, "Intermediate ("Parafiscal") Financing Schemes", in: Levin and Schütze, *op. cit.*, and in Kuhlenkamp/Schütze, *op.cit.*
8. It should be noted that the latter has, besides continuing vocational training and retraining, the main task of placing.
9. The contributions from public budgets would thus be very sizeable if the higher-education sector would be included in the system.
10. Report on an Educational Opportunity Bank: Panel of Educational Innovation (1967), Washington D.C.; K. Shell, F. Fischer, D. Foley, A. Friedlaender (1968), "The Educational Opportunity Bank: An Economic Analysis of a Contingent Repayment Loan Program for Higher Education", *National Tax Journal*, Volume 21, p. 2-45. The alternative to such a government-sponsored Educational Opportunity Bank would be loans from private banks which would have to be publicly guaranteed and subsidised – due to the difficulties in the lending market mentioned above.
11. Cf. K.R. Biederman, B.B. Billings (1974), "Income Contingent Loans for Recurrent Education", in S. Mushkin (Ed.), *Recurrent Education, op.cit.*, pp. 279-294.
12. See for details Biederman/Billings, *op.cit.*
13. The original proposal was based on a four-year full-time university study period.
14. See M. Woodhall (1982), *Student Loans: Lessons From Recent International Experience*, London: Policy Studies Institute.
15. Cf. D.M. Windham (1978), "Theory and Policy of Lifelong Learning", in Windham, Kurland and Levinsohn (Eds.), *Financing the Learning Society*, University of Chicago School Review, Vol. 86, No. 3., p. 535.
16. For a discussion of the consequences of the various financing schemes, cf. Timmermann (1983), "Financing Mechanisms and their Impact on Post-Compulsory Education", in Levin/Schütze, *op. cit.*
17. Provided that the interest rate is higher than the rate of inflation.
18. Edding/Boehm/Dybowski, *op.cit.*, p. 153.
19. H. Levin, in Levin/Schütze, *op. cit.*
20. G. Rehn (1978), in Levin/Schütze, *op. cit.*, p. 145

21. K. Shell et al., op. cit.
22. N. Kurland, *op. cit.*, p. 14.
23. It should be noted, however, that the original Edding model excludes the sector of upper secondary and higher education so that different modes of financing would continue to exist.
24. Cf. K. Shell *et al., op. cit.*, p. 41: "The grant programme seems to undermine one of the goals of the Educational Opportunities Bank to make students responsible for their own education".
25. H. Levin, *op. cit.*, p. 22.
26. See M. Woodhall (1978), *Review of Student Support Schemes in Selected OECD Countries*, Paris, OECD.
27. Cf. V. Stoikov, *op. cit.*
28. This, indeed, is the title of Rehn's main outline of the proposed scheme, *op. cit.*
29. Cf. the figures given in K. Shell *et al., op. cit.*
30. Cf. Louis Emmerij, "Paid Educational Leave: A Proposal Based on the Dutch Case", in Levin/Schütze, *op. cit.* It should be noted, however, that this proposal has not been put into practice.
31. Cf. OECD (1976), *Public Expenditure on Education*, Paris.
32. The results were arrived at by assuming an average working life of 45 years. Thus, since everyone would take one year and be paid at full salary, the cost would be 1/45 of the wage bill. Since wages and salaries are about 60-70 per cent of GDP, this would make the cost about 1 1/2 per cent of GDP. If instruction costs are likely to be one third again, the total cost would be about 2 per cent of GDP.
33. In Levin and Schütze, *op. cit.*
34. Edding, Boehm and Dybowski, *op. cit.*, pp. 150-153.
35. This is suggested by Edding *et al., ibid.*
36. An Independent Commission on the Costs and Financing of Vocational Training in Germany (chaired by Friedrich Edding, the principal advocate of parafiscal funding considered in this report) recommended in 1974 the setting up of a Central Vocational Training Fund to expand the supply and ensure the quality of vocational education, which would eventually encompass not only initial training but vocational education for all age groups. Such a recommendation met with stiff resistance from industry and eventually failed – not just because of the increased contributions through levies but because of opposition to greater government influence over vocational education.